Fowey Lifeboats

150 years of gallantry

Nicholas Leach

▲ Fowey lifeboats
14m Trent Maurice and
Joyce Hardy and D class
inflatable Olive Two
at Polkerris in January
2009 to celebrate the
150th anniversary of the
opening of the station.
(RNLI/Nigel Millard)

Published by Foxglove Media,
Foxglove House, Shute Hill,
Lichfield, Staffs WS13 8DB
Telephone 01543 673594

British Library Cataloguing in Publication Data. A catalogue record for this book is
available from the British Library.

ISBN 978-0-9513656-5-6
Layout and design by Nicholas Leach. Printed by Gutenberg Press, Malta.

Acknowledgements • Thanks to Paul Richards, Captain Will Mitchell, Coxswain Keith
Stuart, Sam Ellis, Tamsin Thomas, Tim Stevens, Dave James, and, at the RNLI, Brian
Wead, Valerie Kirch, Eleanor Driscoll and Nathan Williams.

Contents

Introduction

The coastline of Cornwall has a reputation for being one of the most treacherous in Britain. The small town of Fowey lies on the county's south-east coast, overlooking a picturesque river estuary which provides a deep-water harbour. Situated between Plymouth and Falmouth, and ten miles north-eastward from Dodman Point, Fowey is the largest of the china clay ports developed on this coast during the late eighteenth and early nineteenth centuries.

The modern lifeboat station at Fowey celebrated its 150th anniversary in 2009, with life-saving in the area having begun with the establishment in the 1850s of the Polkerris lifeboat station. Pulling lifeboats manned from Fowey and launched in the small cove have given way to modern motor lifeboats, and today the 14m Trent Maurice and Joyce Hardy and the D class inflatable Olive Two are ready to help those in difficulty off Cornwall's south coast with the volunteer crew ready to put to sea 24 hours a day, 365 days a year.

◄◄ Maurice and Joyce Hardy has served at Fowey since 1996. (RNLI/Nigel Millard)

The station is one of more than 230 managed by the Royal National Lifeboat Institution (RNLI) throughout the United Kingdom and Republic of Ireland, and funded entirely by voluntary contributions. In the south-west in 2008, the RNLI's 35 lifeboat stations launched 1,567 times, rescuing 1,671 people and spending more than 2,150 hours at sea on emergency call-outs alone. The RNLI's annual running costs are over £122 million, approximately £335,000 per day.

▼ Map of Fowey and the adjacent coastline, with the small village of Polkerris to the west. (Reproduced from Ordnance Survey map data by permission of Ordnance Survey)

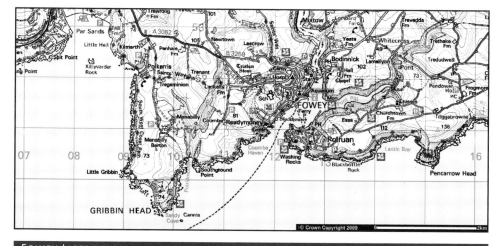

The station at Polkerris

The coast of Cornwall has a reputation for being one of the most treacherous and dangerous for the seafarer who has to pass it or enter one of the county's many ports or harbours. During the eighteenth and nineteenth centuries many lighthouses were built to improve navigation including, in 1795, the first lighthouse to mark the Longships reef, just off Lands End. The major hazards off Cornwall, such as the Wolf Rock, have since been marked by lighthouses and today more lighthouses are operated on the Cornish coast than on any other coast in Britain. The first lifeboat in the county was stationed at Penzance in 1803 and, in March 1824, the Royal National Institution for the Preservation of Life from Shipwreck (RNIPLS) was established to be responsible for 'the preservation of lives and property from shipwreck'. This encompassed the funding, building, operation, maintenance and organisation of lifeboats and lifeboat stations.

The first rescue in the Fowey area noted in the RNIPLS' Minute Books took place in August 1826 when the seine boat Providence, of Par, manned by eight men, was driven onto the rocks during a gale outside Polkerris Harbour. All eight men aboard were thrown into the sea and were being carried away by the tide when Lieutenant Else, RN, of the Polkerris Coastguard, with five of his men, manned a 14ft Coast Guard punt and managed to rescue them. For his efforts, Else was awarded the Gold medal by the RNIPLS.

▶ On Gribbin Head, a mile and a half south-west of Fowey harbour entrance, Trinity House agreed to build a daymark to distinguish that headland from its neighbours. From its base, the daymark stands 84ft high and 250ft above high water mark. Painted in red and white horizontal bands on three sides and white on the landward side, it was erected in 1832 by Trinity House of Deptford Strond. (Paul Richards)

Another rescue, in 1829, also received recognition from the national body. Five men from the seine boat Diligence were saved by the Commissioned Officer Thomas Cresswell, of Polkerris Coastguard, who put out in a local boat to reach the casualty. At a meeting of the RNIPLS Committee on 14 October 1829 the Silver medal was voted to Cresswell for his bravery.

Although the RNIPLS provided some new lifeboats in Cornwall, by the 1840s the organisation's efforts started to falter through lack of funds. However, in the 1850s the Institution was reformed, renamed

◀ The village of Polkerris, on the north-eastern shore of St Austell Bay, with the first lifeboat house visible at the end of the small road leading to the beach. This is almost certainly the first lifeboat house built when the station was established in 1859. (Supplied by Paul Richards)

the Royal National Lifeboat Institution (RNLI), and began to make new public appeals. A new design of lifeboat, the self-righter, was developed and, with greater funds available, lifeboat provision was improved.

In Cornwall, many new stations were established and, in the mid-1850s, a lifeboat station to cover the Fowey estuary and St Austell Bay was established. The founding of the station at Polkerris came about following a tragic wreck on 6 May 1856 in which three men died when their vessel, the schooner Endeavour, of Ipswich, was wrecked near Gribbin Head during an easterly gale. Although Captain George Norcock, Commander of the Coastguard, arrived on the scene to find the vessel smashed to pieces and three of her four crew dead, he manned a boat which was lowered down the 200ft cliff to bring the one survivor ashore. The RNLI awarded Silver medals to Norcock and the two men who helped him, Thomas Henwood and Richard Johns, for their efforts.

When the report of this wreck was given to local landowner William Rashleigh, he wrote to the RNLI asking for a lifeboat to be supplied. With strong local support, the RNLI agreed that a station should be established and a lifeboat provided. However, deciding upon the best site for a station proved impossible. Although Fowey was the obvious choice because of its large population of seafarers, the harbour entrance was such that a pulling and sailing lifeboat could not get to sea during onshore gales. No decision was made for three years until Rashleigh ensured that further funds would be sent to the RNLI to resolve the matter. Then, the village of Polkerris, to the west of the river Fowey, was chosen as the most suitable site for the station.

A small 30ft, eight-oared lifeboat was allocated to the station. Rashleigh contributed

Catherine Rashleigh	
On station	November 1859 – 1866
Record	6 launches, 33 lives saved
Donor	Fund of the Hon Mrs Rashleigh
Dimensions	30ft x 7ft x 3ft 3in
Type	Self-righter, eight-oared
Cost	£136
Builder	1859, Forrestt, Limehouse
Disposal	Decayed, broken up 1867

► One of the earliest photographs of a Polkerris lifeboat, this picture probably shows the station's second lifeboat, Rochdale, on her carriage at Par. The exact occasion is not known but is most likely some ceremonial event as the three persons at the boat's stern are not part of the crew and so may be about to go for a trip aboard the craft. (Supplied by Paul Richards)

£50 of the £300 it cost to establish the station, gave a site on which a lifeboat house could be built, and supplied stone for the new building. His wife donated a further £50, while the local MP, T. J. Agar Robartes, gave £25. The new lifeboat reached Polkerris after being brought by rail to Lostwithiel, then rowed down the river to Fowey, around Gribbin Head, and to Polkerris. Afterwards she went around the bay and was seen at Par and Charlestown by large crowds. The new lifeboat was named Catherine Rashleigh after Rashleigh's wife. A boathouse was built at the top of the beach by Lamerton at a cost £138 4s. For the first year of its operation, the lifeboat was launched over skids. However, in 1860 a carriage was supplied to make launching easier, as well as enable the boat to go by road to Par if necessary.

During her seven years on station, Catherine Rashleigh was launched six times on service, and is credited with saving thirty-three lives. She undertook a fine rescue on 11 June 1862 after the Danish schooner Sylphiden, of Nakskov, was caught in a heavy southerly gale. The vessel was sheltering under the cliffs east of Polkerris when she attempted to run for Par harbour. When the anchors were let go again, the vessel was blown into shallow, broken water, so her crew fired distress signals. The lifeboat soon reached the ship and lifeboatmen went aboard to take the ship into Polkerris. It was brought safely inside the pier, close to the lifeboat house, and according to the local newspaper report, 'in a manner which reflects the greatest credit on Mr Stabb, the coxswain and the crew of the lifeboat.' Such gallantry did not

Rochdale and Catherine Rashleigh

Renamed	1873 – Rochdale 1879 – Arthur Hill
On station	November 1866 – 1887
Record	7 launches, 13 lives saved
Donor	Rochdale LB Fund/ 1879- Arthur Hill Memorial Fund
Dimensions	32ft x 7ft 5in x 3ft 3in
Type	Self-righter, ten-oared
Cost	£262
Builder	1866, Forrestt, Limehouse
Disposal	Sold 1891

go unrewarded and, for his part in this rescue, Coastguard Chief Officer Stabb was accorded the Institution's Thanks Inscribed on Vellum.

The last services performed by Catherine Rashleigh took place on 25 November 1865 when she helped two vessels. In the early morning she went to the brig Wearmouth, of Sunderland, in strong south-westerly hurricane force winds. Following the brig a few miles behind was a barque, Drydens, of North Shields. They made for Par harbour, but both struck Par Sands and were stranded. The waves were breaking over their top masts and their crews were in considerable danger.

Catherine Rashleigh, with Chief Boatman Joshua Heath in charge, was launched but, as she headed to the vessels, she was hit by a heavy sea which swamped her and four oars were carried away. Coxswain Heath was forced to make for Par Harbour, and on seeing the lifeboat apparently sailing away, the crew of the brig launched their own boat but, as one man boarded it, the rope broke and the boat was carried away. The lifeboatmen saw this mishap, and managed to reach the boat just in time to save its occupant. Continuing on to Par Harbour, the lifeboatmen landed the survivor, and his cat, and got new oars. They then made for the barque and, on reaching it, took off the thirteen crew before heading for Par where the rest of the survivors were landed.

The lifeboat again put out, this time for the brig. Although the gale had worsened, the lifeboat reached it, took off her crew of nine and landed them at Par Harbour. The lifeboat reached Par accompanied by, according to the West Briton newspaper, 'the ringing shouts of the joyous spectators on the pierhead'. The brig was badly damaged and later became a total wreck. The barque, carrying maize, went to pieces and came ashore on Par Beach. Following this outstanding double rescue, the Silver medal was awarded to Coxswain Heath.

Not long after this medal-winning rescue, Catherine Rashleigh was found to be suffering from rot, so a new and larger lifeboat was ordered. The new boat, its carriage and alterations to the boathouse were funded by monies raised in the city of Rochdale. To meet the wishes of both the lifeboat station's supporters and the fund-raisers, the new boat was given a double name, Rochdale and Catherine Rashleigh, although this was shortened to Rochdale in 1873.

In 1879 the lifeboat was renamed Arthur Hill after a retired headmaster of Brice Castle School, Tottenham, in London. A fund had been presented to Mr Hill as a testimonial on his retirement and he decided to give it to the RNLI to buy a lifeboat. As no new boat was then available, the name was temporarily carried on the 1866 lifeboat until Polkerris received a new lifeboat in 1887. The final service performed by this lifeboat took place on 18 November 1885 when she went to the Goole schooner Tam O'Shanter, which had been caught in a heavy easterly gale. The lifeboat stood by the vessel until the wind moderated.

The last lifeboats at Polkerris

► Arthur Hill on her launching carriage with the crew in cork life-jackets and shore helpers ready for the launch. She served at Polkerris from 1887 to 1904 and saved four lives. (Supplied by Paul Richards)

A new lifeboat was sent to Polkerris in November 1887. She was a standard 34ft self-righting type incorporating the latest improvements in lifeboat design. These included water ballast tanks, one or more of which could be filled with or emptied of water within a minute. The water ballast increased the weight of the boat and increased stability without adding any extra weight when the boat was being launched. If capsized, the boat would right and be clear of water in a short time. The new Arthur Hill lifeboat arrived in 1887, while the 1866-built boat was removed and four years later sold out of service.

Arthur Hill was, like her predecessor, funded from the Arthur Hill Memorial Fund. She served at Polkerris until 1904 during which time she was launched only three times, and completed just one effective service. This took place on 22 December 1895 in dense fog and a heavy gale. In a break in the fog, at about 5.30am, a flare was seen and the lifeboat, with the already crew standing by, launched within a few minutes, setting a course for Callyvarder Rock. Here they found the schooner Emily, of Padstow, with a cargo of granite. She was anchored close to the shore and unable to work her way out of the bay due to the prevailing wind. The lifeboat crew feared the cable would break, so they took off the four crew and landed them safely.

The next lifeboat to be stationed at Polkerris,

Arthur Hill	
Official Number	136
On station	November 1887 – March 1904
Record	3 launches, 4 lives saved
Donor	Arthur Hill Memorial Fund
Dimensions	34ft x 7ft 6in x 3ft 10in
Type	Self-righter, ten-oared
Cost	£406
Builder	1887, Forrestt, Limehouse
Disposal	Broken up April 1904

the last before operations moved to Fowey, was James, William and Caroline Courtney, one of the Watson class, regarded at the time as the most up-to-date design. Designed principally for sailing, Watson type lifeboats were intended to increase the area covered by the stations from which they operated. Designed by and named after George Lennox Watson, the RNLI's consulting naval architect, the design was broader than the self-righting types and offered much better stability, although was not self-righting.

This new lifeboat was 35ft in length, and drew 1ft 9in of water when her ballast tanks were empty. She cost £1,241 and the carriage, which was fitted with Tipping's wheel plates, a further £250. These plates, the invention of Lt Cdr Tipping, consisted of sets of seven iron plates bolted around the outside of the large rear wheels of the carriage. As the wheel turned, two of the plates were always beneath the wheel, preventing the carriage from sinking into the sand. To accommodate the larger lifeboat, a new, larger lifeboat house was built at a cost of £863.

The formal inauguration and naming of the new lifeboat was held on 25 May 1904 when she was dedicated by the Rev S. V. Baker, vicar of Tywardreath, after which Lt Howard Rowley, RN, District Inspector of Lifeboats, handed over the new boat and boathouse. The Branch Chairman, Evelyn W. Rashleigh, accepted them, and Miss Rashleigh christened the boat James, William and Caroline Courtney by launching her into the water, and officially opened the new lifeboat house.

During her eighteen years at Polkerris, James, William and Caroline Courtney performed four effective services as well as several launches that did not result in rescues. The first service took place on 12 February

▼ Naming ceremony of James, William and Caroline Courtney in May 1904. The lifeboat can be seen on her carriage on the slipway outside the lifeboat house being launched with the crowd dressed in their 'Sunday best'. Tipping's plates fitted to the carriage's wheels helped the carriage to cross soft sand without sinking. (Supplied by Paul Richards)

▶ Launch of the 35ft Watson James, William and Caroline Courtney from the lifeboat house. This photo was probably taken during an exercise launch and shows the slipway down which the boat had to be pushed to launch. (Supplied by Paul Richards)

1907 when the brigantine Adelaide, of Fowey, carrying a cargo of coal, began dragging her anchors in a gale. One of the cables parted but the other held, keeping her clear of the rocks just off the harbour entrance. At 2.30am James, William and Caroline Courtney was launched by which time, the brigantine had grounded and started to bump heavily in the shallow water. When the tide ebbed the situation eased and, with the intention of saving his vessel, the captain asked the lifeboat to send for a tug. The tug Gallant arrived from Fowey and, at about 7am, took Adelaide in tow. Four lifeboatmen were put on board the casualty to help with the pumps, and she was beached safely at Polruan inside Fowey Harbour.

On 5 October 1909 the schooner Wilm, of Fowey, left Par with a cargo of china clay bound for Kirkcaldy, when the wind dropped off Gribbin Head and she started to drift ashore near the Little Gribbin. Signals of distress were fired but on receiving no answer, the crew of five men put off in the ship's boat for Par to obtain assistance. Arriving there at 12.30am, the rockets were fired for the lifeboat, and James, William and Caroline Courtney was soon launched with the crew of Wilm on board. The lifeboat reached the schooner soon after 2am but, despite an extensive search, no sign of Wilm was found. The lifeboat sailed to Fowey to seek further information and those on board were surprised to find Wilm moored in the harbour. The lifeboat crew later learnt that the tug Gallant had left Fowey as soon as the rockets had been fired and put three of her own crew on board Wilm. They had weighed her anchor and the tug towed her into Fowey.

On 30 May 1913, the schooner Alma, of Bremen, was driven ashore on Crinnis Beach in a strong south-westerly gale on passage from Newhaven to Par. James, William and Caroline

James, William & Caroline Courtney

Official Number	515
On station	April 1904 – 12 August 1922
Record	8 launches, 2 lives saved
Donor	Legacy of Mrs C. Courtney, Exmouth
Dimensions	35ft x 9ft x 4ft 11in
Type	Watson, ten-oared
Cost	£1,241
Builder	1904, Thames IW, Blackwall
Disposal	Sold August 1922 for £100

Courtney was launched just after 2pm and stood by as the captain and crew of five were taken off by the coastguard's breeches buoy. On returning to Polkerris, the lifeboatmen found the French schooner Volontaire at anchor in a dangerous position near the small breakwater. The schooner's captain refused their advice and did not require any assistance, so they returned to Polkerris. The lifeboat was not rehoused but left at moorings to be ready should the schooner need help.

At 4.45pm, the schooner's cables parted, she drifted close to Polkerris pier, and stranded on the beach nearby. The coxswain and one of the crew boarded the lifeboat and, by means of ropes, manoeuvred close to the stranded vessel. The French crew again refused assistance, so the lifeboat was hauled back to her mooring. Within a few minutes, however, the crew began climbing down the schooner's bow to try and wade ashore through heavy surf. The lifeboatmen went into the water to help and, although most of the schooner's crew reached the shore unaided, two fell into the water and had to be saved by the lifeboat crew.

The last two services performed by the Polkerris lifeboat both took place in 1914. At 5.30pm on 24 May the lifeboat went to an open boat which was in difficulties nine miles from Polkerris. A few minutes before the lifeboat could reach the man, however, he was picked up by HMS Squirrel and was transferred to the lifeboat. The second service, and the last by a Polkerris lifeboat, took place on 4 November. Late in the evening of 3 November, the schooner Abeja, of Exeter, was reported ashore on rocks near Gribbin Head. At 1am on 4 November James, William and Caroline Courtney launched and found the schooner on rocks. Because of the state of the tide nothing could be done to tow her off, and both lifeboat and tug had to wait. On the turn of the tide, the tug succeeded in towing the schooner off the rocks and towed it to Polruan where, although it was leaking badly, it was safely beached.

▼ Launch of James, William and Caroline Courtney in the early years of the 20th century. This photograph clearly shows the small village of Polkerris, and was taken from the small breakwater which provided the launchers with a degree of shelter when getting the lifeboat afloat. (Supplied by Paul Richards)

Transferred to Fowey

Both the location and naming of the lifeboat station to cover St Austell Bay and the coast to the east of Fowey were issues debated and discussed at various times. In 1905, the question of moving to Fowey was brought up following the loss of the brigantine Mary, of Milford, on 31 December which resulted in the loss of three lives during a south-easterly gale. The brigantine was wrecked at the entrance to Fowey Harbour and, in less than five minutes, had disappeared from sight. The captain managed to jump on to a ledge of rocks from where he was rescued by William Penrose, whose brothers, Thomas and Henry, had lowered him on a rope down the cliff. For this rescue, William Penrose was awarded the Silver medal by the RNLI and the Thanks Inscribed on Vellum was accorded to the others.

In February 1906 the matter of a lifeboat at Fowey was discussed at length at a committee meeting, but no agreement could be reached as to whether the station should stay at Polkerris, move to Fowey, or whether another lifeboat should be placed at Fowey. Four years later, however, the matter was again raised. In February 1910 Henry Arthur Paull, Honorary Secretary of the Fowey Mercantile Association and manager of the Fowey Steam Tug Company, wrote to the RNLI that Polkerris was unsuitable for the lifeboat station and that an enquiry into the matter should be held.

In April 1910 various RNLI Inspectors visited Fowey and could not see any need for a change of location as the station at Polkerris was operating efficiently, had recently had money spent on it, and the large expenditure on a new station at Fowey could not be justified.

The Polkerris station was heavily influenced by Fowey and this is reflected in its official name. The principle source of financial backing came from the Fowey Branch of the RNLI and when it first opened, the station was known as Fowey. However, the name came to be something of a contentious issue. Between 1892 and 1895, it was more accurately known as Polkerris, but from 1895 until 1903 the title Polkerris and Fowey was used. This was more satisfactory to those involved, particularly as the fund-raising branch was operated at Fowey and known as the Fowey and Polkerris Branch.

James, William & Caroline Courtney	
Official Number	394
On station	24 July 1922 – November 1926
Record	3 launches, 0 lives saved
Donor	Legacy of Mrs C. Courtney, Exmouth
Dimensions	40ft x 10ft 4in
Type	Self-righter, twelve-oared
Cost	£649
Builder	1896, Hansen, Cowes
Career	Built as Civil Service No.4 and served at Walmer 1897-1912 and Selsey 1919-22; sold out of service in March 1927

In 1904, the name again reverted to Polkerris and this was used until 1922, when the station actually moved to Fowey.

Manning the lifeboat was generally not a problem despite Polkerris being a fairly small village. The population was itself insufficient to provide enough manpower for the lifeboat, so other men who lived at Fowey were also on the crew, while the majority lived at Par to the west. A firing post was erected at Par in 1893 to summon them and, later the same year, a flagstaff placed on the East Cliff for signalling to Par and the coastguard. This improved matters and was one of a number of initiatives to improve communications at this time. The gradual introduction of telephone communications also helped matters, and in April 1906 a telephone was installed in the Honorary Secretary's house connecting it to the coastguard stations at Par.

The outbreak of the Great War in 1914 affected the operation of the lifeboat service in a number of ways: first, the manpower available diminished; and second, the application of technology was held up. In south-east Cornwall, the number of horses on farms dwindled and towards the end of the War pushing poles were provided to help launch the lifeboat from the beach at Polkerris. Pushing poles were commonly used on the east coast of England to help get the lifeboat to sea through heavy surf breaking on an open beach, but were less common on the west coast where carriage launching was an easier and more practical alternative. When the poles were used in conjunction with the haul-off warp, launching could be satisfactorily achieved.

▼ The lifeboat house built on the beach at Polkerris in 1903 which was used until the station closed in 1922. It was converted into a cafe and shop with the old service boards displayed inside. (Nicholas Leach)

In 1904 the first motor lifeboat had entered service with the RNLI, and during the War the Institution announced a ten-year plan for motorising the entire lifeboat fleet would be initiated once the War had ended. By the end of the War, the long-term future of the station at Polkerris was somewhat uncertain. The RNLI's Annual Report for 1919 proposed a self-righting motor lifeboat for Polkerris, but as a design of light, carriage-borne motor lifeboat was not yet available, a motor lifeboat would have to be moored in open water outside Polkerris Pier. Having considered the scheme, it was decided that Fowey would be the best place for a motor lifeboat as it could provide sheltered moorings needed.

In 1922 the Polkerris station was closed and James, William and Caroline Courtney was sold out of service. She was subsequently converted into a twin-screw motor yacht, renamed Grey Fox, registered at Exeter and initially used along the south coast. The lifeboat house built in 1903 was converted into the Lifeboat Café, and remains so today, with the old service boards inside. On the closure, a number of retiring awards were made: a pension was given to William Cauker, who had served as Bowman for seven years and Coxswain for five; a gratuity went to Sidney Robins, who was five years as Second Coxswain; and a pension was granted to W. H. R. Hawken, who had been signalman for 16 years.

When the station was moved to Fowey in 1922, the RNLI's lifeboat building programme had been delayed by World War I so a reserve self-righting pulling and sailing lifeboat, rather than the expected motor lifeboat, was supplied. This reserve lifeboat was, like her predecessor at Polkerris, named James, William and Caroline Courtney having been appropriated to the legacy of Mrs Caroline Courtney, of Exmouth. Unlike her predecessor, however, she was a self-righter, 40ft in length, pulling twelve oars, and was kept afloat at moorings in the river. Originally named Civil Service No.4, she had been built in 1896 for Walmer where she had saved 155 lives. After leaving Walmer in 1912, she was placed in the reserve fleet and served at Selsey, amongst other places, before coming to Fowey. She arrived at Fowey from Southampton on 11 August 1922, and stayed for four years.

The new lifeboat was only launched three times while at Fowey and did not save any lives. The first launch took place on 3 August 1923, during the Saturday afternoon sailing race for cruisers outside the harbour. A strong wind was blowing from the west, when the yacht Nancy disappeared as she was about to round the western mark. Rockets were fired from the coastguard station to alert the lifeboat, which was immediately launched to search for the

William Roberts

Official Number	505
On station	December 1926 – August 1928
Record	0 launches, 0 lives saved
Donor	Legacy of William Roberts, Manchester
Dimensions	40ft x 11ft x 5ft 4in
Type	Watson, twelve-oared
Cost	£1,606
Builder	1903, Thames IW Blackwall
Disposal	Condemned 1928

missing yacht together with the other yachts that were participating in the sailing race. The tug Cruden Bay, an ex-trawler owned and operated by the Fowey Steam Tug Company, also joined the search, but unfortunately no trace of the yacht or its occupants was found, and the search was eventually called off. The bodies of the Nancy's crew were recovered a week later.

During the night of 12 November 1926 the schooner I. M. Nielson, of Svendborg, ran on to the rocks near Polperro and was holed. James, William and Caroline Courtney set out and began tacking eastward against a strong south-easterly wind. As the lifeboat reached the wreck, the coastguards on the cliff signalled to the lifeboatmen to return as the schooner had already broken up. Five of the schooner's crew, who were wearing life jackets, had been washed ashore. When close to the shore, they were assisted to safety by coastguards and fishermen who had gone into the surf. However, one of the crew, who had jumped onto a rock from the schooner's bowsprit, could not be reached by the coastguards. He was in danger of being struck by the masts of the wreck as waves threatened to cover the rock. Although pitch dark, local fisherman Joseph Curtis volunteered to go down the cliff to rescue the stranded man and both were hauled up the cliff to safety. As a result of his bravery, Curtis was accorded the Thanks on Vellum by the RNLI.

In 1926, James, William and Caroline Courtney was replaced by a Watson of a similar size named William Roberts. Built for Littlehaven in Pembrokeshire in 1903, where she served until April 1921, this lifeboat had later served in the reserve fleet at both Southend-on-Sea and Aberdeen before coming to Fowey on 2 December 1926. She was a 40ft Watson sailing lifeboat, equipped with twelve oars. During her time at the station, she was not called upon for any service launches, and proved to be the last sailing lifeboat to serve at Fowey.

▼ A view over the harbour mouth at Fowey, showing one of the sailing Watson lifeboats at moorings near the Town Quay amongst a cluster of small dinghies and yachts. (Supplied by Paul Richards)

C. D. E. C.

◀ The 45ft 6in Watson motor lifeboat C. D. E. C. pictured during her naming ceremony. She was powered by twin 40hp Weyburn CE.4 four-cylinder engines which gave her a maximum speed of just over eight knots, a radius of action of sixty-one nautical miles at full speed and seventy-eight nautical miles at cruising speed. In total, she carried 112 gallons of fuel. (Supplied by Paul Richards)

During the first decade of the 20th century the RNLI began to develop motor lifeboats. Although crews in pulling and sailing lifeboats often performed remarkable feats of life-saving, a powered lifeboat provided distinct advantages over one relying on sails and oars. In 1904 a lifeboat was fitted with an engine for the first time. Although many technical problems had to be overcome to successfully operate an engine on board a lifeboat, once they had been solved motor powered lifeboats began to be built and within two decades motor power had become a vital element in life-saving.

Further developments with motor lifeboats were delayed by the War of 1914-18, but once this was over the RNLI made up for lost time by embarking upon an ambitious building programme. The first motor lifeboats in Cornwall were stationed at the Lizard in 1918 and at St Mary's in 1919 and, during the years between the two World Wars, motor lifeboats were sent to ten Cornish lifeboat stations.

The first motor lifeboat to serve at Fowey was the 45ft 6in Watson cabin type H. C. J., which served as a temporary lifeboat after the pulling lifeboat William Roberts had been found unfit for further service and condemned in August 1928. In order to provide cover, H. C. J., which was on passage to Thurso, the station for which she had been built, was diverted to Fowey in late August. She stayed at the station until December by which time the station's own motor lifeboat, C. D. E. C., had arrived. H. C. J. then continued on to Holyhead and lastly Thurso.

The new motor lifeboat's name, C. D. E. C., was somewhat unusual. It was made up of the initials of the names chosen by the persons whose legacies had been amalgamated to meet the £8,300 cost of construction. The four donors were Mr C. G. Nottage, of London; the late Miss G. E. Moss, of Liverpool; the late Mrs J. Liddell, of Wadebridge; and the late Mrs A. S. Picking, of London.

The new lifeboat was named and dedicated at an inaugural ceremony in blazing sunshine on 4 September 1929, during Fowey regatta week. Many people gathered at Whitehouse and small craft surrounded the lifeboat as she lay at Whitehouse slip for the formal handing over and dedication, presided over by the Mayor of Fowey, Councillor George Chatworthy. The platform was in the front part of the garden of The Haven, the residence of Sir Arthur Quiller Couch. After a prayer by the vicar of Fowey Reverend W. R. Guest, Lieutenant Colonel C. R. Satterthwaite, OBE, the RNLI's Deputy Secretary, presented the lifeboat to the Fowey Branch. She was accepted by the Mayor of Fowey who then invited Mrs Treffry to name the lifeboat with the traditional champagne bottle smashed over her bow.

The motor lifeboat had a much greater operating range than its man-powered predecessors. Consequently, the Fowey lifeboatmen could cover a larger area with their new lifeboat which, during more than a quarter of a century at the station, performed more than sixty services and is credited with saving just under fifty lives. The following descriptions cover the main rescues performed by the lifeboat during her time at Fowey, two of which had been performed before her official naming ceremony, although neither resulted in effective services.

The first, on 18 April 1929, was to the French liner Paris, owned by Compagnie Transatlantique which, with 1,500 people on board, was due to call at Plymouth en route from Le Havre to New York. After running aground on the Eddystone Rock, the liner radioed for help and, as the Plymouth lifeboat was out of action, C. D. E. C. put out, slipping her moorings at 12.22pm, just four minutes after the maroons had been fired. On arrival at the Eddystone, the crew were informed by the lighthouse keepers that Paris had already refloated, so the lifeboat returned to Fowey without having provided any assistance. The second service took place on 12 May 1929, when C. D. E. C. was involved in an unsuccessful search for a 70-year-old retired naval engineer whose motor boat had broken down off Dodman Point.

The next significant launch by C. D. E. C. took place on the evening of 20 August 1930 to the 43ft cutter yacht Islander, on passage from Dartmouth to Falmouth, which got caught in a

H. C. J.	
Official Number	708
On station	August – December 1928
Record	0 launches, 0 lives saved
Donor	Legacies of H. T. Richardson and Mrs S. Stephens; and gift from Mr John A. Fielden
Dimensions	45ft 6in x 12ft 6in x 6ft 3in
Type	Watson motor
Cost	£8390 0s 9d
Builder	1928, J. S. White, Cowes
Career	Transferred to Holyhead and Thurso, sold out of service 1962

south-easterly gale with a very heavy sea and rain. The yacht was last seen near the bell buoy marking the Udder Rock off Lanivet Bay. A member of a camping party in Lanivet Bay, a Dr Fox, was walking on the cliffs when, at 8.30pm, he saw what resembled a flare from near the Udder Rock and alerted the Polruan Coastguard. The coastguard immediately called out the lifeboat and C. D. E. C. left her moorings straight away.

Although initially the lifeboatmen had some difficulty in locating Islander, after half an hour the lifeboat's searchlight picked out the yacht, which was stranded less than 200 yards from the cliffs. The lifeboat was taken as close as possible and anchored in an attempt to reach the casualty from the sea. Meanwhile, the life-saving apparatus team had arrived and transported their equipment to the cliff top where they set it up. The first rocket they fired missed the casualty but, before a second rocket could be fired, Islander was lost from sight by the life-saving team. Out at sea, the lifeboatmen fired a rocket line towards the casualty but it fell short. More of the lifeboat's anchor cable was paid out in a dangerous attempt to get closer, but the lifeboatmen were too late as the yacht was driven onto the rocks.

Once it became clear that the lifeboat could not give any further assistance, two men climbed down the cliff and, taking a rope from a boat drawn up in a cove, managed to get on to Island Rock. The yacht, with her mast broken, was now being slowly but surely swept towards the rock. The men on shore could hear cries for help and could make out six persons on board, five of whom were huddled together motionless. Three more men joined the two already on Island Rock but, before anything could be done, a heavy sea struck the yacht and carried it away from the shore, parting the anchor cable. The yacht then struck a reef and sank leaving only the mast visible. All six on board were washed away and drowned despite the rescuers making every effort to help.

A Board of Trade enquiry into the tragedy was held at Fowey Town Hall. The enquiry's report made various recommendations about the coast-watching system, but did not find the lifeboat crew or the station's Honorary Secretary at fault for having arrived on the scene too late. The report was critical of the fact that one of the coastguard huts, that at Lantivet, was not manned at the time of the incident. In bad weather, such as prevailed at the time Islander was lost, the Lantivet hut, as well as the coastguard huts at Polperro and Portwrinkle, should have been manned by coastguard officers who could keep watch.

C. D. E. C.	
Official Number	712
On station	December 1928 – Nov 1954
Record	65 launches, 49 lives saved
Donor	Legacies of C. G. Nottage, London; G. E. Moss, Liverpool; Mrs J. Liddell, Wadebridge, and A. S. Picking, London
Dimensions	45ft 6in x 12ft 6in
Type	Watson motor
Cost	£8,309 6s 3d
Builder	1928, J. S. White, Cowes
Disposal	Sold out of service November 1959 for £1,120

The report found that 'The organisation and system of the coastguard Service in operation were not efficient for the purpose of maintaining an efficient look-out . . . and had not provided for the proper manning of all the stations at which a look-out was necessary in the weather conditions prevailing.' To the five men who had risked their lives climbing down the cliff to offer assistance, the Board of Trade made various awards.

On 5 September 1934 C. D. E. C. was involved in the rescue of the occupants of a small motor boat. Two men and two women hired a motor boat, Ken, to go to a beach on the west side of Lantic Bay. When the boat neared the beach, a heavy swell carried it onto the rocks and it was stranded at the foot of an almost sheer cliff. One of the men managed, with difficulty, to climb the cliff and go for help. As soon as the alarm was raised, C. D. E. C. set out with a small boat in tow. Once on scene, three lifeboatmen manned the small boat and managed to rescue the two women and the man.

The first wartime rescue by C. D. E. C. took place on 4 January 1940 after distress signals had been fired from a vessel off Mevagissey. C. D. E. C. slipped her moorings and headed out into a very heavy sea and poor visibility. The lifeboat found the 5,000-ton steamship Ardangorm, of Glasgow, stuck fast on the Gwineas Rock with heavy seas breaking over her. Coxswain Jack Watters told the ship's captain that his ship would be safe until daybreak, when the lifeboat would rescue him and his crew.

After standing by throughout the night, the lifeboat was taken alongside the steamship from which eleven men were saved. The survivors were landed at Fowey and two tugs were requested to help

▼ C. D. E. C. at her usual moorings with the town's picturesque waterfront providing the backdrop. (Supplied by Paul Richards)

▶ C. D. E. C. at moorings off the Town Quay. (By courtesy of Paul Richards)

refloat the vessel. The lifeboat returned to the casualty and stood by until 2.30pm. Meanwhile, an Admiralty tug arrived but it was decided to abandon the steamer as there was no hope of saving her. The lifeboat therefore took off the remaining men, twenty-five in number, and returned to her station at 4.15pm.

The dangers of wartime service were demonstrated on 4 November 1940 after Motor Gun Boat (MGB) 40 detonated an acoustic mine just off the entrance to Fowey harbour. The MGBs were based at Fowey, and each week one was sent to Plymouth to clear any acoustic mines which had been dropped by enemy aircraft in Plymouth Sound. The high speed MGBs were well clear when the mines were detonated by the sound of the boat's engines. However, on the occasion in question, MGB 40 was returning to Fowey from her week at Plymouth when, on slowing down near the harbour entrance, she accidentally detonated a mine which left her very badly damaged. C. D. E. C. arrived on scene, exploding three more mines without damage to herself, to offer assistance. However, the crew of MGB 40 was rescued by MGB 46, which went out through the harbour at over forty knots. MGB 40 was later towed into the harbour.

As with all of Britain's lifeboats, the war years were difficult for the lifeboat at Fowey. Not only did ships become stranded or wrecked through following irregular courses, but many lifeboat crew members joined either the Navy or Army. The coast was unlit, mines added to the dangers while enemy submarines were active off Cornwall and the south coast of England. Despite spending many hours at sea, often searching for missing vessels, C. D. E. C. actually performed few effective services.

The final wartime call for the lifeboat was on 11 August 1945 when, at 12.58am, the police reported that a yacht was missing. The yacht, with five people on board, had left the previous afternoon but had not returned. Just over a quarter of an hour after the police call, C. D. E. C. was launched. She located the yacht three miles south of Polruan and towed her safely back to Fowey, where both boats arrived at 4.45am.

In the first year of peace, C. D. E. C. performed two services. The first was to a sailing dinghy, on 21 July 1946, which had capsized near Punches Cross, at the eastern side of the harbour entrance. The dinghy's two occupants had got ashore safely on their own, so the lifeboat towed the dinghy back to Fowey. The second took place on 27 November when she went to the steamship Valborg, of Copenhagen, to help pilot her in. However, the master refused help, saying the weather was too bad to safely bring his ship into port. The following day the ship again signalled for a pilot, and this time the lifeboat escorted the steamer into harbour.

In 1947 the reserve lifeboat The Brothers was on station while C. D. E. C. was being overhauled, and she was involved in one of the station's most outstanding rescues. On the morning of 23 March 1947, the coastguard reported signals of distress in Par Bay. The weather was very poor with a south-westerly force seven wind blowing, accompanied by very heavy seas. The Brothers was launched at 4.40am and, under Coxswain John Watters, her crew searched the Bay but without success. After almost an hour a small light was seen near Callyvarder Rock. As the lifeboat approached, her crew saw that the light was coming from a hand torch held by one of a group of men on a sunken vessel. All that could be seen were the vessel's bows and poop, and the midship section was under water. The ship, the motor vessel Empire Contamar, a former German war prize, was bound from Maryport to Par with a cargo of coal. She had gone ashore at 1.30am after her anchors had dragged. The bad visibility had shrouded her distress signals for three hours.

As the tide was rising and threatening to engulf the casualty, it was essential for the lifeboatmen to make a quick rescue. The coxswain tried to get alongside under the bow, but the seas were too heavy. He therefore made an approach bow first, intending to fire a line to the men sheltering on the poop, but the first attempt

▼ C. D. E. C. at her regular moorings off the Town Quay in April 1936. (From an old photo by Grahame Farr)

was unsuccessful. At the second attempt, the lifeboat was washed over the sunken rail into the waist of the ship and, although she was washed out again, some damage was done to her bows. The lifeboatmen succeeded in throwing a line aboard and, using this, were able to haul the seven men, soaked through and frozen, to safety. The rescued men sheltered in the lifeboat's cabin while the lifeboat made best speed to Fowey. For this difficult and perilous rescue, which had been undertaken in heavy seas and total darkness, Coxswain Watters was awarded the Bronze medal, and the crew received additional monetary awards.

On 15 January 1950 C. D. E. C. was launched in a choppy sea with a fresh south-westerly wind to go to the assistance of a fishing boat with a motor boat in tow. The fishing boat Prim was found with an ex-RAF tender in tow. The tow rope had parted and fouled the fishing boat's propeller. As the boat's crew of two were unable to cut the tow away or make headway under sail, the lifeboat took both boats in tow and brought them safely back to Fowey harbour.

During 1954, the Fowey lifeboat undertook eleven launches of which three resulted in effective services. The first took place on 3 July 1954, when C. D. E. C. assisted the local motor launch Acorn, which had broken down off Blackbottle Head. The last call of the year took place in the early hours of 2 September, and this proved to be the last service performed by C. D. E. C. as station lifeboat at Fowey. The fishing lugger Ibis, of Mevagissey, with a crew of three, had gone ashore at Great Perhaver Beach. C. D. E. C. put out at 2.30am in a calm sea and fog, stood by Ibis until she refloated on the tide and then escorted her into Mevagissey. In November 1954, a new lifeboat was placed on station at Fowey, so C. D. E. C. was reallocated to the RNLI's Reserve Fleet in which she served until being sold out of service in November 1959.

▼ The Reserve lifeboat White Star off the Town Quay. (Paul Richards)

Deneys Reitz

◀ 46ft 9in Watson motor lifeboat Deneys Reitz on trials shortly after being built, with an open steering position amidships. She served Fowey for more than a quarter of a century. (Supplied by Paul Richards)

The new lifeboat, a 46ft 9in Watson cabin class with midship steering, a cabin forward and a shelter on the after deck, was named Deneys Reitz. Powered by two 40bhp Ferry VE4 four-cylinder diesel engines, the lifeboat's top speed was 8.41 knots. She had a cruising speed of 7.5 knots and a radius of action of 164 nautical miles at this speed. She could carry 120 people in calm weather, or 95 in rough conditions. During her time at Fowey, various alterations and additions were made to her: her wheelhouse was enclosed to provide improved crew protection, and her original engines were replaced by two 70hp Watermota Sea Lion engines in 1970.

She was built by Groves and Guttridge, Cowes, and the Fowey crew travelled to Cowes to collect the new boat. She was brought to Fowey after an eleven hour passage under Coxswain Jack Watters and Motor Mechanic Bill McDonald. Funds had come from the Southern Africa Lifeboat Fund, which had been established by the RNLI's South Africa Branch and collected funds in Southern and Northern Rhodesia, Nyasaland, the Bechuanaland Protectorate and Swaziland, as well as South Africa. Its first appeal was made in 1940, organised by Miss Pattie Price, and it eventually raised sufficient money to buy three lifeboats.

The first of these, a 46ft Watson motor, was named Field Marshall and Mrs Smuts and

Deneys Reitz	
Official Number	919
On station	November 1954 – May 1980
Record	155 launches, 36 lives saved
Donor	South African Branch of RNLI
Dimensions	46ft 9in x 12ft 9in
Type	Watson cabin motor
Cost	£31,922
Builder	1954, Groves & Guttridge, Cowes
Disposal	Sold out of service 1980, used as a pilot boat out of Sheerness; later refitted as a cabin cruiser, renamed Joy M, then Daniel Arthur, and used for cruising

served Beaumaris from 1945 to 1977. The second lifeboat funded by the South Africa Branch was a 51ft Barnett named Southern Africa, which served at Dover from 1949 to 1967. The third and final boat to come from the fund was sent to Fowey and named Deneys Reitz after an officer who fought against the British in the Boer War, and served on the allied side fighting on the Western Front during World War I. He later became an important figure in South African politics during the inter-War years.

The new lifeboat's inauguration ceremony was held on 6 July 1955 and for the ceremony the lifeboat was moored off the Town Quay, which was crowded with hundreds of people. Mrs Pattie Price, who had played a large part in raising the funds in South Africa, handed over the lifeboat to Colonel A. D. Burnett Brown, Secretary of the RNLI. He then handed her over to Major D. R. Carter, Honorary Secretary. The boat was dedicated by the Rev T. H. Elkington, Vicar at the Missions to Seaman at Fowey, with the assistance of the Vicar of Fowey.

At the end of the ceremony, the lifeboat was christened by Mrs Jooste, wife of the South Africa High Commissioner and the guests were taken for a short trip. The minesweeper HMS Bramble was moored near the lifeboat and her Commanding Officer, together with some of his officers, attended the ceremony. The lifeboat was manned for the naming ceremony by Coxswain Jack Watters, Second Coxswain Wally Stephens, Motor Mechanic Bill McDonald, Bowman Harry Pearse, Second Mechanic Jim Turpin, Ross Bennett, Bill Stephens and Del Davies.

▼ The scene at the Town Quay during the naming ceremony of Deneys Reitz on 6 July 1955. (Supplied by Paul Richards)

◀ Reserve lifeboat Cecil and Lilian Philpott at moorings off Fowey Town Quay while she was standing in for Deneys Reitz in 1966. She was built in 1930 and served for almost thirty years at Newhaven before a decade in the Reserve Fleet. She was sold out of service in October 1969. (Paul Richards)

◀ Reserve lifeboat John R. Webb, built in 1930, served in the Reserve Fleet from 1955 to 1969 before being sold out of service. She was at Fowey from June to August 1960 performing three service launches.

Deneys Reitz, while at Fowey, launched 155 times on service, and is credited with saving thirty-six lives. Before her inauguration she was called out on five occasions, but the only effective service took place early on the morning of 23 March 1955. She left the harbour at 5.45am and headed out into a rough sea and south-westerly gale to go to the motor vessel Festivity, of London, which was in difficulty on the eastern side of St Austell Bay. The lifeboat found Festivity dragging both her anchors, so stood by until the wind moderated. Festivity then weighed her anchors and, escorted by the lifeboat, made for Fowey harbour.

On 12 September 1958 Deneys Reitz assisted in a difficult situation that resulted in the station's assistant mechanic being formally rewarded for his efforts. The coastguard at Charlestown had gone to help a young woman who had been cut off by the tide west of Charlestown, but it was impossible to haul the girl up the cliffside so the lifeboat was called. At 5.32pm Deneys Reitz left her moorings and, after a line had been fired ashore, the Assistant Mechanic swam ashore to make the line fast to a rock. The girl and a coastguardsman, who had gone to help her, were taken off by breeches buoy and landed at Fowey. For his efforts during this difficult rescue, the Thanks inscribed on Vellum was accorded to Assistant Mechanic James Turpin.

In 1959 the station's centenary was celebrated, marking 100 years of the lifeboat station at Polkerris and Fowey. A ceremony was held on 7 December 1959 in the Council Chamber. Lieut-Cdr H. H. Harvey, the RNLI's District Inspector, presented a Vellum to the Mayor of Fowey, Alderman A. L. Evans, after Major D. R. Carter, the Honorary Secretary, outlined the history of the station during which the Fowey and Polkerris lifeboats had launched 144 times on service and saved 114 lives.

On 7 March 1963, Deneys Reitz was called on to help the Danish motor vessel Idalith, which had gone ashore while attempting to enter Par harbour. As a southerly gale was imminent, Deneys Reitz put out at 1am on 8 March in very rough seas to stand by Idalith until the vessel refloated under her own power soon after 4am. The lifeboat then escorted her back to Fowey.

On 24 July 1966, a self-drive motor boat was swamped a few miles off Fowey and the four passengers were thrown overboard. They were rescued by another boat and brought into Fowey harbour. One of the survivors, Mrs Frances Hogan, was unconscious so Mechanic Frederick (Mike) Webber helped to treat her. He got the mouth to mouth resuscitation apparatus from the lifeboat and some blankets. The apparatus was used for about thirty minutes and the woman revived.

▼ A fine photograph of Deneys Reitz taken towards the end of her service career when she had a fully enclosed wheelhouse and had been fitted with radar. She served at Fowey from 1954 to 1980. (Jim Matthews)

Mechanic Webber was later awarded with the Royal Humane Society's resuscitation certificate.

In summer 1966, a tragic accident occurred off the south Cornish coast when, despite the best efforts of lifeboatmen from Fowey, Coverack, Falmouth and Salcombe, many lives were lost. On 31 July the pleasure boat Darlwyne, a 45ft former Admiralty picket boat, left Falmouth with a crew of two and twenty-nine passengers for a day trip to Fowey. The weather when she departed was good, although the forecast suggested gusty winds along her route. She reached Fowey without incident and, about three hours later, set out on the return journey. Soon after leaving Fowey, the weather deteriorated. Between 5pm and 6pm a vessel was seen heading towards Dodman Point, but no more was seen of Darlwyne or the thirty-one people aboard her.

By the early hours of the morning, Darlwyne had been reported overdue and at first light on 1 August Deneys Reitz and the Falmouth lifeboat Crawford and Constance Conybeare began to search for the missing craft. Deneys Reitz searched an area to the east of Dodman

◀ James Turpin, who was appointed Coxswain in 1958, had been on the crew since 1938 and ten years later became Assistant Mechanic. He is one of the best known of all Fowey lifeboatmen and served for forty years in total, retiring in 1978. In 1977, he was presented with the BEM, an award which he formally received from the Lord-Lieutenant of Cornwall, Lord Falmouth. (By courtesy of the RNLI)

◀ Deneys Reitz at moorings in the harbour. This photo shows her with an enclosed wheelhouse and radar. (By courtesy of the RNLI)

Point, while the Falmouth lifeboat searched to the seaward, aided by an RAF Shackleton aircraft. During the afternoon, a dinghy was found, believed to have come from Darlwyne. Fowey and Falmouth lifeboats abandoned their search at 9pm having found nothing, and the following morning Salcombe lifeboat The Baltic Exchange searched for more than five hours, together with William Taylor of Oldham, the Coverack lifeboat, but without success and nothing was found.

On 4 August Crawford and Constance Conybeare put out in the early hours of the morning after wreckage had been sighted four miles east of Dodman Point. Deneys Reitz was also launched, and she recovered two bodies, a harrowing task for the lifeboat crew, as well as some wreckage which was believed to have come from Darlwyne. The bodies were transferred to the Falmouth lifeboat, which had arrived on the scene, so Deneys Reitz could continue with the search. The sea was so choppy that the transfer was too difficult and one of the bodies had to remain on the Fowey lifeboat while the Falmouth lifeboat returned to land the other bodies. The search continued throughout that day but nothing more was found, so Deneys Reitz returned to station.

In total, twelve bodies from the pleasure craft had been found by 16 August. Each had drowned in deep water and, using information about the last sightings, attempts were made to find the scene of the wreck.

▼ An excellent photograph of Deneys Reitz off the harbour. She served at Fowey for more than a quarter of a century and is one of the station's best remembered lifeboats. (By courtesy of the RNLI)

◀ Relief 46ft Watson motor lifeboat Gertrude at moorings in the harbour during her time as temporary station boat. (Paul Richards)

Although Royal Navy divers located more than 900 underwater objects belonging to the vessel, the hull of Darlwyne was never found. The major cause of the disaster was Darlwyne putting to sea when she was not fit to withstand the normal conditions which she might expect to encounter. However, despite attempts to find out what happened, the exact events that resulted in Darlwyne sinking were never established.

On 1 December 1975 the 800-ton Danish coaster Elizabeth Boye went ashore on the rocks at Spit Beach, near Par Harbour. The coaster began to drag her anchor when the wind freshened to gale force eight, and she was broadside on to the rocks when the alarm was raised. Deneys Reitz launched at 7.25am and a helicopter from RNAS Culdrose was quickly on scene. Five of the coaster's crew were winched to safety by the helicopter despite rain and high winds. Because of the deteriorating weather, the helicopter returned to base while the lifeboat stood by. The lifeboatmen got a line aboard the ship as the skipper, using his engines, got the ship clear of the rocks. The ship was then driven onto the beach, where she was inspected for damage. The lifeboat worked the towline to the ship, keeping her stern straight out to sea. As the tide rose the lifeboat began to pull and, just after 11am, the coaster slid free.

The final service performed by Deneys Reitz at Fowey took place on 23 August 1979, when she saved a speedboat and its three occupants, and in May 1980 she left the station for the last time. During more than a quarter of a century of service, she had performed in excess of 150 service launches, and is credited with saving thirty-six lives. She was sold out of service in 1980, and remained unaltered during the 1980s as a houseboat in Falmouth. Renamed Joy M and then Daniel Arthur, she has now reverted to her original name and is used as a pleasure boat.

As a new lifeboat had not yet been allocated to the station to replace her, a series of relief lifeboats were sent for temporary duty. The first was Gertrude, a 46ft Watson, built in 1946, which had served originally

▶ Relief 46ft Watson Jesse Lumb at the moorings off the Town Quay. This lifeboat served at Bembridge from 1939 to 1970, and then spent more than a decade in the Relief F leet including a spell at Fowey in 1975. (Paul Richards).

at Holy Island. She was stationed at Fowey until November 1981 during which time she performed four routine services and saved two lives.

The most significant rescue performed by Gertrude at Fowey took place on 10 May 1981. She was launched to the 28ft yacht Christina, which had been driven onto the rocks near Fowey during the afternoon. The yacht had been making for Fowey when a force five wind had driven her towards cliffs between Coombe Beach and St Catherine's light. The two people on board could not start the engines and were helpless as the yacht went onto the rocks. They scrambled ashore when Polruan coastguard cliff rescue team arrived and helped take off equipment. Later the lifeboat fired a line ashore and a tow rope was rigged to the yacht. As the tide rose during the evening, the lifeboat pulled Christina from the rocks and towed her to Fowey.

On 25 November 1981 the 46ft 9in Watson Guy and Clare Hunter was sent to the station. Newer than Gertrude, she had been built in 1955 and served for more than twenty-five years at St Mary's, saving 110 lives. Less than a month after Guy and Clare Hunter had been on station, and before she had performed a service, the Penlee lifeboat Solomon Browne was tragically lost on service on 19 December 1981 to the motor vessel Union Star with the loss of her entire crew of eight. While the nation as a whole was stunned by this incident, the depth of the tragedy was felt particularly throughout Cornwall's lifeboat communities. In the aftermath of the tragedy, Guy and Clare Hunter was transferred to Penlee from Fowey. She was deemed most suitable to operate from the Penlee boathouse, where she would be launched down the slipway, as her rudder arrangement had been designed with this practice in mind for her service at St Mary's.

Gertrude	
Official Number	847
On station	May 1980 – November 1981
Record	8 launches, 2 lives saved
Donor	Legacy of Lady Struthers
Dimensions	46ft x 12ft 9in
Type	Watson cabin motor
Cost	£17,048
Builder	1946, Rowhedge Iron Works, Rowhedge
Career	Originally at Holy Island; sold out of service in February 1983 and kept at Mevagissey

◀ Relief 46ft 9in Watson Charles Henry Ashley moored at Fowey Town Quay in 1982. (Peter Gudmunsen)

At Fowey, in place of Guy and Clare Hunter came Charles Henry Ashley, a 1949-built 46ft 9in Watson similar to Deneys Reitz, which had served at Porthdinllaen from 1949 until 1978. She arrived on 25 January 1982, and served until being replaced in October that year by a new lifeboat. She performed only two services during 1982, both routine ones to pleasure craft that had got into difficulties.

▼ Relief 46ft 9in Watson Charles Henry Ashley at the harbour entrance. (Paul Richards)

Leonore Chilcott

▶ Leonore Chilcott
approaches the Town Quay
for her naming ceremony,
with relief Brede Merchant
Navy at moorings.
(Paul Richards)

During the early 1980s the RNLI developed a new class of lifeboat designated the Brede, based on a commercially-designed hull. At 33ft in length, it was regarded as an 'intermediate' lifeboat because, although larger and more capable than an inshore lifeboat, it was smaller than other offshore lifeboat types and was restricted in the worst weather conditions. The first of the Bredes, operational number 33-01, was never named and used only for trials before being sold. The second, 33-02, had a larger wheelhouse than the first, an arrangement employed on the Bredes which went into service. The third Brede, 33-03, named Leonore Chilcott, was allocated to Fowey and became the first to go on station when she became operational on 16 October 1982.

The Brede lifeboat was based on the Lochin 33, a craft designed by Robert Tucker and originally built for use as a commercial angling boat. It was developed and built by Lochin Marine at Rye, Sussex, and was given the class name Brede after the river which forms a tributary of the river Rother which flows through Rye. The hull was constructed of moulded glass-reinforced plastic and the watertight wheelhouse provided a self-righting capability. The boat was powered by twin 203hp Caterpillar 3208NA diesel engines which gave a top speed of twenty knots and a range of 140 nautical miles at full speed.

Leonore Chilcott	
Official Number	1083
On station	October 1982 — January 1988
Record	57 launches, 19 lives saved
Donor	Gift of Paul Chilcott, Channel Islands
Dimensions	33ft x 12ft
Type	Brede
Cost	£153,475
Builder	1982, Lochin Marine, Rye
Disposal	Sold out of service Sept 1990

◄ Paul Chilcott on board the lifeboat he funded. Born in Devon, he knew Fowey and the surrounding area well, so it was fitting that the lifeboat he had funded should be stationed there. He had watched the boat being built and had been on her sea trials. (By courtesy of the RNLI)

Before the new lifeboat was sent to Fowey, Coxswain Brian Willis, Mechanic Keith Stuart and crew members Peter Gudmunsen and Bill Taylor spent ten days familiarising themselves with the new craft at Poole under the direction of the RNLI's South West District Inspector Les Vipond. The new boat went to Weymouth and then crossed to Jersey where, after exercising with the St Helier lifeboat, took the donor of the boat, Paul Chilcott, back to Guernsey from Jersey. The lifeboat arrived

▶ Fowey's new lifeboat, Leonore Chilcott, showing her speed off Charlestown following a publicity visit, September 1983. (Paul Richards)

at Fowey at the beginning of October 1982 and, after a week of crew training, she was placed on station.

The new lifeboat had been funded by Mr Chilcott's in memory of his late wife, and was named and dedicated at a ceremony on 26 April 1984 at the Town Quay, watched by hundreds of people. The dedication service was conducted by the Bishop of Truro, the Right Reverend Peter Mumford, assisted by the Reverend David Woods, Vicar of Fowey and the Reverend Ian Morris, Vicar of Lanteglos-by-Fowey. At the end of the ceremony, Mr Chilcott formally christened the new lifeboat by breaking the traditional champagne bottle over the bow.

Leonore Chilcott served at Fowey for only six years, during which time she saved nineteen lives. She was fairly busy performing numerous services to dinghies, yachts and other pleasure craft, and she launched a total of fifty-seven times on service. During a service on 19 July 1983 her speed proved vital when she went to the Plymouth-registered fishing vessel Abraham Cove, which had taken in water, capsized and sunk nine miles south-east of Fowey. The vessel's crew had taken to their life raft after attempts to save their vessel failed, and had been picked up by another fishing vessel, Pescado. The men were transferred to the lifeboat and landed at Fowey at 6.44pm.

In the summer of 1985, the relief lifeboat Merchant Navy, on station in place of Leonore Chilcott, performed several routine services to pleasure craft. One took place on 13 July after the 30ft sailing sloop Magpie II suffered a machinery failure in the vicinity of Gwineas Rocks. Merchant Navy was launched to assist as the single occupant of the yacht was seventy years old and unable to sail the vessel. The lifeboat proceeded to the casualty and towed it safely into Mevagissey. During the return trip to Fowey, the starboard engine failed. At the station, one of the engine's filters was changed and sea trials were satisfactorily carried out.

On 26 June 1986, Leonore Chilcott was launched in gale force winds and rough seas to the yacht Jillamanda II. Manned by a crew of six under the command of Coxswain Willis, the lifeboat left her moorings at 11.10pm and was operating at her limit. The yacht had suffered engine failure and was in danger in the difficult conditions, but the lifeboat brought it safely to Fowey where her crew of two were landed.

On 31 August 1987 Leonore Chilcott was launched at midday to a sinking yacht close to Polruan. Despite the conditions being beyond her operating limits, the lifeboat left the safety of the harbour. Within three minutes of the lifeboat putting to sea, the casualty began sinking. The lifeboat reached the vessel, the 26ft sloop Vreny, and went alongside so the lifeboat crew could go aboard to pump and bail out the water. Salvage pumps were put on board and the yacht was brought into Fowey harbour. This rescue was undertaken in conditions outside the lifeboat's operating limits and so, partly as result of this service, a decision was taken to allocate an all-weather lifeboat to the station.

During 1987, her final year on station, Leonore Chilcott was involved in several services. One of these occurred on 24 February, when she launched to search off the Dodman between St Austell and St Mawes for the crew of a Sea King helicopter from RNAS Culdrose which had crashed into the sea. She put to sea at 8.40pm and returned the following morning at 5.30am with one of the helicopter's crew still missing. A large search had been undertaken involving many vessels, but little was recovered.

▼ 33ft Brede Leonore Chilcott on exercise in July 1986. (Peter Gudmunsen)

Thomas Forehead and Mary Rowse II

▶ The scene at Town Quay on 26 April 1988 during the rededication of the 44ft Waveney Thomas Forehead and Mary Rowse II. The service was carried out by the Rt Rev Peter Mumford, Lord Bishop of Truro, and was attended by a large number of well wishers and supporters of the station. (Paul Richards)

A lthough the 33ft Brede was effective in most sea conditions, it was an intermediate lifeboat and was restricted in the worst weathers. An all-weather lifeboat was needed at Fowey and so, in 1987, the 44ft Waveney class Thomas Forehead and Mary Rowse II was allocated to the station. Built in 1974 for Plymouth, she had served there for almost fourteen years during which time she had launched 181 times on service and saved ninety-one lives.

The Fowey crew, under the command of John Unwin, RNLI Divisional Inspector South-West, brought the boat to Fowey from the RNLI Depot at Poole, via Weymouth and Alderney, in December 1987. She arrived on 20 December and was greeted at the harbour mouth by relief Brede lifeboat Amateur Swimming Associations and the pilot boat Gore Point. After the crew had been fully trained in the operation and handling of the new lifeboat, she was placed on station on 26 January 1988.

The Waveney was based on a United States Coast Guard design for a 44ft steel-hulled lifeboat and was the first design of 'fast' lifeboat to serve in UK waters. As such, it represented a radical departure from the RNLI's

Thomas Forehead and Mary Rowse II	
Official Number	1028
On station	January 1988 – October 1996
Record	169 launches, 35 lives saved
Donor	Legacy of Thomas Field, Liverpool
Dimensions	44ft 10in x 12ft 8in
Type	Waveney
Cost	£100,000
Builder	1974, Groves & Guttridge, Cowes
Career	Originally at Plymouth 1974-88, sold out of service 1999

◀ Thomas Forehead and Mary Rowse II exercising in a heavy swell off Fowey harbour, December 1987. (Peter Gudmunsen)

traditional designs. Self-righting by virtue of its inherent buoyancy, it was designated the class name Waveney after the river close to the Brooke Marine boatyard where the first six were built for the RNLI. The boat that was stationed at Fowey was the tenth of the class, and was powered by twin 260hp General Motors 8V-53 diesel engines.

Thomas Forehead and Mary Rowse II was rededicated at a ceremony on 26 April 1988 at the Town Quay. In fine weather, a crowd of more than 400 guests and supporters of the station, including Paul Chilcott, donor of Leonore Chilcott, were in attendance to see the Right Reverend Peter Mumford, Lord Bishop of Truro, perform the rededication. Ross Carter, chairman of the Fowey and Polkerris Branch, opened proceedings, and the lifeboat was handed into the care of the Fowey station by Lt Cdr Jeremy Tetley. She was accepted by Captain Roy Pritchard, Honorary Secretary, after which the Rt Rev Mumford, assisted by the Vicar of Fowey, the Rev David Woods, conducted the service.

▼ Thomas Forehead and Mary Rowse II at moorings off the Quay. (Nicholas Leach)

One of the first services performed by the Waveney took place on 3 November 1988. At 3.55pm a small yacht was seen in difficulty with no mainsail about half-a-mile from Fowey. A small motor cruiser was with the yacht, which was beam on to a heavy easterly swell and force eight winds. By 4.05pm the cabin cruiser appeared to have broken down and the yacht was unmanned so Thomas Forehead and Mary Rowse II launched. A red flare was fired from the motor cruiser and, just eight minutes later, the lifeboat was alongside the casualty.

The Waveney picked up the single occupant of the motor cruiser, which sank ten minutes later, and then towed the yacht in to Fowey harbour. The unusual circumstances of the rescue were due to the fact that the yacht, which had been on a single-handed passage from Brittany, had found the abandoned motor cruiser in mid-channel and taken it in tow. The yacht's skipper then found himself in difficulties, and had attempted to tow the yacht with the cruiser, but had problems initially caused by a broken tow-line and then by engine failure. The station's Deputy Launching Authority, Captain Mike Mitchell, was praised for his vigilance and ordering the pre-emptive launch, which saved time. His efforts were recognised by a letter of thanks from the RNLI's Chief of Operations.

In April 1990, Thomas Forehead and Mary Rowse II was away from station for overhaul at Tom's Boat Yard, at Polruan, and in her place was the relief 44ft Waveney Faithful Forester. This lifeboat performed a number of routine services in April and May, and made the national news headlines following a service on 20 June when the Prime Minister, Margaret Thatcher, was on board. Mrs Thatcher was at the station

▼ A dramatic photograph of Thomas Forehead and Mary Rowse II hitting a swell off Fowey harbour. (Marcus Lewis)

◀ 44ft Waveney Thomas Forehead and Mary Rowse II at her moorings up the river Fowey, outside Berrill's Yard. (Nicholas Leach)

meeting crew and personnel and went for a trip in the lifeboat. Towards the end of the demonstration, a yacht was seen nearing the port, shipping water and in need of assistance. The lifeboat immediately put out to the casualty, Slipshod, and escorted it to safety. The yacht was not in serious difficulty, and her crew of five, from Southampton, were unaware they were being watched by the Prime Minister. Throughout the operation, Mrs Thatcher was in the wheelhouse alongside Coxswain Stuart.

Thomas Forehead and Mary Rowse II returned to station on 8 July 1990 and performed a number of routine services throughout the remaining months of 1990 and into 1991. On 12 May 1991, she again went away for routine maintenance work, this time to Mashford's Yard at Plymouth, and the relief 44ft Waveney Faithful Forester took her place once more, remaining for just over two months.

During the summer of 1992, the relief 44ft Waveney Faithful Forester was again on duty at Fowey and she performed four rescues during August. The first, on 12 August, was to the fishing vessel Satanic which had two persons on board and was taking in water fast, sinking on her mooring. The lifeboat used its pump to pump out the casualty, which took two hours. The lifeboat then towed the casualty to the boatyard at Polruan.

▼ Thomas Forehead and Mary Rowse II brings in a capsized speedboat in November 1989. (Paul Richards)

Thomas Forehead and Mary Rowse II returned to station in November 1992. During June 1993 she completed three rescues, the first on 3 June. At 3.03pm that day, she put out to the cabin cruiser Trojan, which had broken down

near Mevagissey. On reaching the cabin cruiser, the lifeboat took it in tow to Mevagissey harbour. Three days later, the lifeboat went to the assistance of nine persons stranded on the cliffs under the Carlyon Bay Hotel, in St Austell Bay. The lifeboat reached the area just before 7pm and took seven persons on board, while a helicopter airlifted two persons off the cliff. The third and final service of the month took place on 19 June when the lifeboat launched to two persons stranded on a cliff at Polridmouth Cove. The lifeboatmen reached the scene at 3.13pm and, using a rubber dinghy, two crew members went ashore. They lowered the stranded persons down the cliff and took them to the lifeboat, which returned to Fowey where they were landed.

On 25 July 1993, Thomas Forehead and Mary Rowse II was tasked to go to two persons cut off by the tide west of Lantic Bay. The two persons and their boat were picked up off the rocks, and were taken to Polruan Quay. Two days later the lifeboat was again in action, launching at 7.50pm after four youths in a small inflatable failed to arrive at their destination. The four survivors were found on a beach under Little Gribbin Head suffering from exposure, and their dinghy had been ripped down one side. They were taken on board the lifeboat, treated for hypothermia, and landed at Fowey quay.

On 22 August 1996 Thomas Forehead and Mary Rowse II searched for the yacht Timoneer after one of its two occupants had been washed overboard in severe weather.
Plymouth lifeboat City of Plymouth

▼ Looking towards the Town Quay with, centre right, the building used as a crew facility when the lifeboats were moored off the Quay from 1922, when the station first moved to Fowey, until 1995. (Nicholas Leach)

◀ Thomas Forehead and Mary Rowse II returns to harbour bringing in the broken down pleasure boat Lytham Green on 17 April 1994. (Paul Richards)

was also launched to help with the search, and air-sea rescue helicopters from RNAS Culdrose and RAF Chivenor were scrambled. At 2.15pm the coastguard had picked up a VHF radio message saying 'Help – help me' and immediately tasked the rescue services. The message came from a 13-year-old boy, who was terrified after his father had fallen overboard from the yacht, which was taking on water in heavy seas.

The missing yachtsman was seen in the water by the helicopter from Culdrose and was winched into the helicopter, where attempts to revive him unfortunately failed. Meanwhile, the Fowey lifeboat had found the yacht with its sole occupant. One lifeboatman boarded the casualty, which was then taken in tow. The boy remained on the yacht during the passage to Fowey, and he was taken to the lifeboat house where he was treated for shock. Deputy Coxswain Dave Gammons performed very well during this service, not only managing the boat but also looking after the young boy who was extremely frightened by his ordeal. Gammons stayed with the boy until social services arrived.

At the time of this service, a new Trent class lifeboat, Maurice and Joyce Hardy, was under construction for the station. The last service performed by Thomas Forehead and Mary Rowse II during her time as station lifeboat at Fowey took place on 8 September 1996, when she brought a cabin cruiser and its five occupants to safety. Her final duty as Fowey lifeboat was to host HRH The Duke of Kent just over a week later during the Duke's tour of four lifeboat stations on Cornwall's south coast. He had called at Marazion, Lizard and Falmouth before Fowey.

A week later, the new Trent class lifeboat arrived and Thomas Forehead and Mary Rowse II left Fowey. She was placed in the Relief Fleet, in which she only served for a year. In December 1997, she was withdrawn from RNLI service and, in 1999, was sold out of service to the Royal New Zealand Coastguard Federation. Renamed Westgate Rescue, she became a lifeboat on New Zealand's North Island.

Inshore lifeboats

In 1996 an inshore lifeboat (ILB) was sent to Fowey. Although ILBs had been in service with the RNLI since the 1960s, an inshore craft to cover St Austell Bay had hitherto not been deemed necessary. However, by the mid-1990s, a requirement for inshore cover was identified and so a suitable site had to be found. The ILB, known as the D class inflatable, first entered the RNLI fleet in 1963, and was refined and developed making it an ever more effective and essential life-saving tool.

The 16ft inflatable lifeboats, made from nylon coated with hypalon, are usually crewed by two or three, powered by a 40hp outboard engine, and can be launched quickly and easily. They are equipped with VHF radio, GPS, flexible fuel tanks, flares, an anchor, a spare propeller, a compass and first aid kit. The ILB's advantage is its speed, both in launching to an incident and when at sea.

Initial investigations to find the best location from where to operate an ILB pointed to Mevagissey, but as no suitable site could be found there it was decided to add an ILB to the Waveney at Fowey, initially on a summer-only basis. In May 1995, the RNLI announced that a D class inflatable would be sent to the station from April until October the following year. Work on installing a launch davit began towards the end of 1995, and by the summer of 1996 all was ready for an ILB.

Inshore lifeboats

On station	Off No	Name	Type
8.1996 – 1997	D-390	Tiger D	Avon EA16
2 – 9.1997	D-433	Marjorie	Avon EA16
9.1997–2007	D-526	Olive Herbert	Avon EA16
28.9.2007–	D-681	Olive Two	IB1

The first ILB, a relief boat named Tiger D (D-390), arrived in August 1996 and was used to train the crew before becoming operational. The ILBs that have served at Fowey are all based on a design developed in 1983 by RNLI staff and built by Avon Inflatables at Llanelli, Wales. The first service performed by the ILB was on 5 August 1996 to the yacht First Choice. Two more effective services were carried out in 1996 and the ILB launched on a further four occasions to incidents where others had already coped or searched but without resultant outcome.

In February 1997, Tiger D was replaced by another relief D class inflatable, Marjorie (D-433). This boat served throughout the summer of 1997 until, in September, the new D class inflatable built for the station became operational. The new boat, Olive Herbert (D-526), was funded by the Olive Herbert Charitable Trust.

At first, the ILB was kept in a small wooden container at Berrill's Yard, near the all-weather lifeboat moorings. The station had moved here from the Town Quay in the mid-1990s. At Berrill's Yard, not only was a launch davit installed for the ILB, but a new berth was provided for the lifeboat. To accommodate the ILB, the RNLI obtained a site near Berrill's yard, on the landward side of the road out of Fowey, for a new shore facility to provide supporting services for the crews of both lifeboats. In May 1996, planning permission for the new facility was granted on the site off Passage Street. Work began on the new building in early 1997 and was completed by the end of the summer.

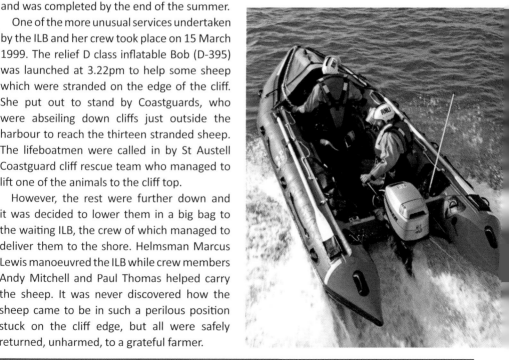

▼ D class inflatable D-526 Olive Herbert on exercise in February 2002. She was one of the first ILBs to have an orange livery as previous ILBs were grey with orange patches. (Nicholas Leach)

One of the more unusual services undertaken by the ILB and her crew took place on 15 March 1999. The relief D class inflatable Bob (D-395) was launched at 3.22pm to help some sheep which were stranded on the edge of the cliff. She put out to stand by Coastguards, who were abseiling down cliffs just outside the harbour to reach the thirteen stranded sheep. The lifeboatmen were called in by St Austell Coastguard cliff rescue team who managed to lift one of the animals to the cliff top.

However, the rest were further down and it was decided to lower them in a big bag to the waiting ILB, the crew of which managed to deliver them to the shore. Helmsman Marcus Lewis manoeuvred the ILB while crew members Andy Mitchell and Paul Thomas helped carry the sheep. It was never discovered how the sheep came to be in such a perilous position stuck on the cliff edge, but all were safely returned, unharmed, to a grateful farmer.

Maurice and Joyce Hardy

▶ The changeover: 14m Trent Maurice and Joyce Hardy is led into harbour by the lifeboat which she replaced, 44ft Waveney Thomas Forehead and Mary Rowse II, September 1996. (Paul Richards)

During the 1990s the RNLI began developing faster all-weather lifeboats incorporating better crew protection with a greater range than any previous lifeboats, as well as building larger and more comfortable shore facilities for the volunteer crews and increasing the number of inshore lifeboats in service, supplying them to stations such as Fowey where an all-weather lifeboat was already operating.

Plans to replace the Waveney lifeboat, which had served Fowey for eight years, were made during the 1990s by which time she and other boats of the class were reaching the end of their operational life. The limitations of the design had become apparent with her relatively slow speed, of only fifteen or sixteen knots, and the open wheelhouse offering inadequate crew protection. To replace the aging Waveneys and Aruns, two new designs of faster all-weather lifeboat, designated Trent and Severn, 14m and 17m respectively, were developed by the RNLI. The new designs used a hard chine hull form, with the hull for the smaller 14m Trent a scaled down version of the 17m Severn's hull. Both boats were self-righting by virtue of the watertight wheelhouse. The engine room was positioned aft, with the Trent's engines staggered so one powers a U-drive and the other a conventional straight drive.

Capable of reaching speeds up to twenty-five knots, almost twice that of the Waveney,

Maurice and Joyce Hardy	
Official Number	1222
On station	10 October 1996 –
Donor	Gift of Maurice G. Hardy CBE, Twyford, Hants
Dimensions	14.26m x 4.53m
Type	Trent
Cost	£1,750,000
Builder	1996, hull moulded by Green Marine, fitted out by Souter Shipyard, Cowes

◀ Fowey lifeboatmen after bringing home the new 14m Trent Maurice and Joyce Hardy: front (crouching, left to right) are Jonathan Pritchard, Ron Johnson, Keith Stuart (Coxswain), Nigel Crowle and Bob Harris; back (standing, left to right) are Rob Husband, Mike Cottrel, Maurice Hunkin, Pat Barron, Marcus Lewis, Mark Monk, Andy Mitchel, Paul Richards and Darren Burt. (Jim Matthews)

the Trent also had a fully enclosed wheelhouse. Both Severn and Trent were built from fibre reinforced composite, a material which combined strength with relatively light weight. The Trent's wheelhouse contained permanent seating for six crew, together with provision for one stretcher in the wheelhouse and another in the forecabin. The hull was subdivided by five bulkheads into six compartments.

The first boats of these new types began entering service in the mid-1990s with a Trent under construction at Souter Shipyard allocated to Fowey. This boat completed her trials in summer 1996 and arrived at Fowey on 25 September that year. Led by Coxswain Keith Stuart, crew members Rob Husband, Jonathan Pritchard, Ron Johnson, Nigel Crowle and Marcus Lewis had been through a week of training at the RNLI's Training Centre in Poole

▼ 14m Trent Maurice and Joyce Hardy and 44ft Waveney Thomas Forehead and Mary Rowse II in the harbour, September 1996. (Paul Richards)

▶ Dressed overall, Maurice and Joyce Hardy with her crew lined up during her naming ceremony on 4 October 1997. (Nicholas Leach)

▶ The scene at Berrill's Yard on 4 October 1997 during the naming and dedication ceremony for the new 14m Trent and D class inflatable lifeboats. (Nicholas Leach)

▶ Maurice and Joyce Hardy leaving harbour after her formal naming ceremony for a short trip with special guests on 4 October 1997. (Nicholas Leach)

since 16 September with the new vessel before bringing her home. On her arrival at Fowey, she was welcomed by a flotilla of small vessels, well-wishers and supporters. On 4 October, she left for a training trip to the Scillies, and six days later was officially placed on service. The new lifeboat had been funded by a gift and bequest from Maurice G. Hardy, CBE, of Twyford and USA, and was named Maurice and Joyce Hardy. Hardy was a keen supporter of the RNLI and, although based in America, had a number of business interests in Cornwall.

The station's new D class inflatable Olive Herbert was placed on station in September 1997 and, with the Trent having been operational for almost a year, the station had two new lifeboats as well as a new crew facility. The official naming and dedication ceremony for the new lifeboats took place on 4 October 1997 when, as part of a unique triple celebration, the Trent and the ILB were christened and the new shore facility was officially opened. Former coxswain Brian Willis opened the new lifeboat house and crew facility.

During the ceremony, Mr D. S. Cattell, a friend of the Hardy family, handed over the Trent lifeboat and Richard Gilman, a trustee of the Olive Herbert Charitable Trust, handed over the D class inflatable. The lifeboats were accepted by David Acland, RNLI Chairman, who delivered them into the care of the Fowey Branch and Honorary Secretary Captain Roy Pritchard. The service of dedication was conducted by the Reverend David Maddock, vicar of Fowey, the Reverend John Halkes from Lanteglos, and Father Robert Draper of St Austell's St Augustine's RC church. At the end of the ceremony, the new Trent was named by Mrs Joyce Hardy, wife of the late Maurice Hardy, and the D class was named by Mrs Stella Welford, a trustee of the Olive Herbert Charitable Trust

On 16 January 1997, the relief 14m Trent lifeboat Earl and Countess Mountbatten of Burma was launched at 3.25pm after a report had been

◀ The inshore lifeboat house and crew facility built in 1997-8 at Berrill's Yard, opposite the lifeboat moorings, on the landward side of the road through the town, with D-526 Olive Herbert outside on her trolley. The new building, funded by a bequest from Marie and George Higginson, of Beverley, Yorkshire, was formally opened on 4 October 1997 as part of the triple dedication ceremony. (Nicholas Leach)

received that a fishing vessel was in distress. The 38ft vessel Heather Ann (FY126) had suffered an electrical fire fifty miles south-east of Fowey, and was unable to start her engine. The lifeboat reached the casualty at 5.35pm and took her in tow to Mevagissey. Both boats arrived at the small port at 11.15pm and once the fishing vessel was safely moored, the lifeboat returned to Fowey, reaching her station just after midnight following what had been a long service. Not long before this service had been undertaken, the RNLI had increased its declared area of coverage from thirty to fifty miles from the shore. The Institution was able to do this following the introduction of the faster all-weather lifeboats such as the Trent. The older, slower lifeboats could not have undertaken a services at such distances as effectively.

In 1998 Maurice and Joyce Hardy and Olive Herbert undertook more than twenty rescues between them. The first launch took place on 4 January and involved an unsuccessful search of the sea off Pentewan Sands near Mevagissey in squally conditions. The first effective service was performed on 9 March when the inshore lifeboat brought two cliff climbers to safety after they had been stranded on cliffs at Appletree Point. During the afternoon of 11 March Maurice and Joyce Hardy was involved in a fruitless search for a wind surfer in difficulties off Polperro.

In 1999, the RNLI celebrated the 175th anniversary of its founding and many events were held up and down the country throughout the year. On 4 March, the anniversary day, the station's Trent Maurice and Joyce Hardy was launched in celebration, the only lifeboat in Cornwall to put

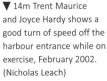

▼ 14m Trent Maurice and Joyce Hardy shows a good turn of speed off the harbour entrance while on exercise, February 2002. (Nicholas Leach)

to sea. A joint exercise was held with a helicopter from RNAS Culdrose, and an anniversary maroon was fired to mark the occasion.

During the anniversary year the station was relatively busy. In the early hours of 17 April, the lifeboats were called out to assist the crew of a yacht which had mistaken the Par river for Fowey harbour. The yacht, Wight Gambit, with two people on board, went aground. Both Maurice and Joyce Hardy and Olive Herbert stood by the yacht and her crew, who chose to stay on board. The lifeboatmen fitted a fender to the stricken vessel to help maintain its buoyancy. Coastguards then dug a pit under the yacht's hull so that she would not fill with water as the tide came in, and at 3.35am the yacht righted, and was then escorted to Fowey.

During 1999, the relief lifeboat Dora Foster McDougall was on station. On 9 August 1999 both Fowey lifeboats were kept busy during a number

◀ Maurice and Joyce Hardy afloat off the Town Quay, prior to an exercise with the local fire brigade. (Nicholas Leach)

of incidents. They launched to five people in difficulty off Par Beach, who were rescued before the lifeboats arrived, but on the way back to station both lifeboats were diverted to assist three people cut off by the tide at Polkerris. During the attempted rescue, the ILB was swamped by the surf and all three crew members were thrown into the water. None was injured, but the boat suffered minor damage. The three people who had been stuck on the rocks managed to scramble to safety with the help of local coastguard teams. On her return to station, Olive Herbert was taken off service due to the damage she had received, and a relief ILB, Ordnance Survey Bosun (D-432) was sent in her place.

On 24 September 1999, at 1.51pm, the lifeboat Dora Foster McDougall was launched following reports that a crew man on board a Russian ship anchored in Par Bay had fallen into the ship's hold. In a fresh south-westerly wind, gusting up to force five, Coxswain Keith Stuart took the lifeboat alongside the casualty, Sormovskiy 3057, and put second Coxswain Steve Barker and crew member Pat Barron to assess the situation, and offer first aid assistance. While this manoeuvre was being undertaken, a search and rescue helicopter was scrambled from RNAS Culdrose with a doctor and a paramedic on board. The helicopter winch them onto the ship where they carried out a detailed examination

▼ Maurice and Joyce Hardy on exercise in the harbour with a Sea King rescue helicopter from RNAS Culdrose. (Paul Richards)

◄ Maurice and Joyce Hardy tows in the yacht Harvard and her crew of three, 9 August 2002. (Paul Richards)

of the casualty before confirming he had suffered no more than bad bruising and could remain on the ship.

The first service for Maurice and Joyce Hardy after an extensive refit took place on 9 January 2000. She was launched at 7.09pm to search for Polperro fisherman Daniel Kebble who, in his 24ft boat, had been reported overdue. The lifeboat led an extensive search, which involved the inshore lifeboat from Looe as well as a search and rescue helicopter, coastguard units from Polruan, Polperro and Looe. A flotilla of local fishing boats also joined the emergency crews. The search went on throughout the night and into the following morning. However, after more than twenty hours at sea, the lifeboatmen reluctantly returned to station having found no trace of the missing fisherman.

During 2001, the relief Trent Inner Wheel II was on station while Maurice and Joyce Hardy was undergoing a routine overhaul. The first call of the year took place on 2 March when the lifeboat went to the aid of the fishing boat Saturn which was taking in water three miles east of Dodman Point. The skipper had called for help when he was unable to contain the water. A rescue helicopter from RNAS Culdrose was first on scene, and lowered a pump on board the vessel. The lifeboat then arrived and, using a second pump, the lifeboatmen were able to get the incoming water under control.

On the morning of 2 February 2002 the Fowey lifeboat was involved in a fine rescue after the 1989-built cargo vessel Kodima, laden with timber, contacted Brixham Coastguard to request help after being caught in very rough seas approximately ten miles south east of Dodman Point. Maurice and Joyce Hardy put out at 5.20am, under Coxswain Keith Stuart, to assist the vessel, which was then twenty-one miles off Fowey. The lifeboat

▶ Maurice and Joyce Hardy at her pontoon berth at Berrill's Yard, with relief 14m Trent Betty Huntbatch berthed astern. Lifeboats on passage and on trials often call at Fowey, sometimes staying overnight. Betty Huntbatch was sent to Hartlepool in September 2004 as station boat. (Paul Richards)

encountered severe conditions on her way to the casualty, which had started to drift in the heavy seas. But she remained intact, although she had developed a heavy list to port in the treacherous conditions. The lifeboat and a helicopter from RNAS Culdrose arrived on scene together, and the crew were taken off by helicopter. The operation was complicated by the severe weather, with a ten metre swell accompanied by a south-westerly force eight to nine wind. The severe conditions tested the lifeboat and her crew to the limit, but they remained standing by until the Emergency Towing Vessel Far Sky arrived.

After drifting, Kodima eventually hit the beach at Tregantle Range, in Whitsand Bay east of Fowey, during the evening of 3 February. A salvage operation then commenced, although the salvors had to contend with heavy weather which hampered their efforts. Once the difficult conditions had been overcome, the vessel was finally freed at 5.22pm on 16 February, two weeks after she had first run aground.

After standing by when the ship first got into difficulties, Coxswain Stuart said 'The conditions were very bad, but the boat performed well. We spend many hours exercising in readiness for events like this and it all pays off when we're called out. Our main role was to stand by while the helicopter winched off the crew. It was an extremely difficult operation given the seas and wind conditions and I take my hat off to the helicopter crew for their expertise.'

On 2 November 2005 Fowey lifeboat was involved in another challenging operation after the merchant vessel Galina, with eight persons on board, lost power just over five miles south-east of Dodman Point and was in danger of being driven ashore in storm force conditions. Falmouth lifeboat also launched, and the Coastguard Emergency Towing Vessel Anglian Princess was tasked to assist. The two lifeboats arrived on scene just after midnight on 3 November by which time the vessel was four miles off Dodman Point with winds gusting to fifty-five knots. With Anglian Princess more than an hour away, action had to be taken to try and reduce the drift. After many attempts to get a line on board, the

Falmouth crew attached a tow to attempt to slow the vessel's drift.

The lifeboat then slowly extended the tow and set a south-easterly course, managing to maintain a speed of one knot against the very rough conditions with breaking seas. Anglian Princess arrived on scene at 2.35am and the towline was passed across to the larger vessel. Fowey lifeboat stood by throughout the operation and was at sea in the very rough conditions for several hours, until being released to return to station after 4am. For his support during this service, Coxswain Keith Stuart received a Framed Letter of Thanks signed by the RNLI Chairman.

On 28 September 2007 a new inshore lifeboat, Olive Two (D-681), was sent to the station. The new ILB was formally named on 4 May 2008. She replaced Olive Herbert (D-526), which served from 30 September 1997 to September 2007 during which time she launched 177 times and saved 149 people. Like her predecessor, the new lifeboat was funded by the Olive Herbert Charitable Trust. The new boat was named by Stella Welford in front of about 400 people. The service of dedication was conducted by the two local vicars, the Rev Philip de Grey-Warter, of Fowey & Golant, and the Rev Louise Courtney, of Lanteglos by Fowey. The ILB had been called out on 3 May, the day before the naming ceremony, to help rescue three teenagers cut off by the tide at Porthpean Beach.

For 150 years the lifeboat crews of Fowey and Polkerris have been ready to go to the aid of vessels in difficulty off Cornwall's south-east coast. Between 1859 and 1922, the Polkerris lifeboats saved fifty-two lives and launched on service twenty-four times. Between 1922 and 31 December 2008, the Fowey lifeboats saved 188 lives and launched on service 660 times. Between 1996 and 31 December 2005, the ILBs saved fourteen lives and launched on service ninety-one times.

▼ The IB1 inshore lifeboat Olive Two (D-681) is put through her paces off Berrill's Yard following her naming ceremony on 4 May 2008. (Tim Stevens)

Lifeboats

On station	Official Number	Name Donor	Dimensions Type	Launches/ lives saved
POLKERRIS LIFEBOATS				
1859 – 1866	—	**Catherine Rashleigh** Fund of the Hon Mrs Rashleigh.	30' x 7' Peake self-righter	6/33
1866 – 1887	—	**Rochdale and Catherine Rashleigh/** 1873 – **Rochdale** /1879 – **Arthur Hill** Rochdale Lifeboat Fund/ 1879 – Arthur Hill Memorial Fund.	32' x 7'5" Self-righter	7/13
1887 – 1904	136	**Arthur Hill** Arthur Hill Memorial Fund.	34' x 7'6" Self-righter	3/4
1904 – 1922	515	**James, William and Caroline Courtney** Legacy of Mrs C. Courtney, Exmouth.	35' x 9' Watson	8/2
FOWEY LIFEBOATS				
1922 – 1926	394	**James, William and Caroline Courtney** Legacy of Mrs C. Courtney, Exmouth	40' x 10'4" Self-righter	3/0
1926 – 1928	505	**William Roberts** Legacy of William Roberts, Manchester	40' x 11' Watson	8/2
8 – 12.1928	708	**H. C. J.** Legacies of H. T. Richardson and Mrs S. Stephens; and gift of Mr J. A. Fielden	45'6" x 12'6" Watson motor	0/0
1928 – 1954	712	**C. D. E. C.** Legacies of C. C. Nottage, G. E. Moss, J. Liddell, and A. S. Picking	45'6" x 12'6" Watson motor	65/49
1954 – 1980	919	**Deneys Reitz** South African Branch of RNLI	46'9" x 12'9" Watson motor	155/36
1980 – 1981	847	**Gertrude** (TSD) Legacy of Lady Struthers	46' x 12'9" Watson motor	8/2
1981 – 1982	926	**Guy and Clare Hunter** (TSD) Legacy of Mrs Hunter, and others	46'9" x 12'9" Watson motor	0/0
1 – 10.1982	866	**Charles Henry Ashley** (TSD) Legacy of Charles Carr Ashley, Mentone	46'9" x 12'9" Watson motor	5/0
1982 – 1988	1083	**Leonore Chilcott** Gift of Paul Chilcott, in memory of his wife	33' x 12'1" Brede	56/19
1988 – 1996	1028	**Thomas Forehead and Mary Rowse II** Legacy of Thomas Field, Liverpool	44'10" x 12'8" Waveney	169/35
1996 –	1222	**Maurice and Joyce Hardy** Gift of Maurice G. Hardy CBE, Twyford, Hants	14.26m x 4.53m Trent	

TSD indicates Temporary Station Duty

Services

Polkerris

Catherine Rashleigh Lifeboat

1862	June 11	Schooner Sylphiden, of Nakskov, saved vessel & 7
1865	Jan 29	French lugger La Mère Françoise, Le Père Samson, saved lugger and 4
	Apr 30	Galliot Eintracht, of Hamburg, stood by
	Nov 25	Barque Drydens, of North Shields, saved 13
		Brig Wearmouth, of Sunderland, saved 9

Rochdale and Catherine Rashleigh (later Rochdale) Lifeboat

1867	Mar 17	Schooner Devonia, of Padstow, saved 5
1872	Mar 27	Galliot Dora, of Amsterdam, saved 4
1873	Feb 1	Schooner Hawk, of Chepstow, saved vessel and 4
1885	Nov 18	Schooner Tam O'Shanter, of Goole, stood by

Arthur Hill Lifeboat

| 1895 | Dec 22 | Schooner Emily, of Padstow, saved 4 |

James, William and Caroline Courtney Lifeboat

1907	Feb 12	Brigantine Adelaide, of Fowey, assisted to save vessel
1909	Oct 5	Schooner Wilm, of Fowey, attempted to put crew on board
1913	May 30	French schooner Volontaire, saved 2
1914	May 24	Small boat of Par, saved boat and 1
	Nov 4	Schooner Abeja, of Exeter, stood by
1915	Jan 1	Unknown ketch, crew assembled but no launch
	Dec 27	Schooner Pedestrian, of Fowey, crew assembled but no launch

Fowey (from 1922)

James, William and Caroline Courtney Lifeboat

| 1926 | Nov 12 | Schooner I. M. Nielsen, of Svendborg, no service |

William Roberts Lifeboat

| | | No services |

C. D. E. C. Lifeboat

1929	Apr 18	Steamship Paris, of Le Havre, no service
	May 12	Motor boat Ripple, of Falmouth, unsuccessful search
1930	Aug 20	Cutter yacht Islander, of London, no service
1931	May 27	Fishing boat Kenneth, of Mevagissey, escorted
		Fishing boat Mac, of Mevagissey, escorted
	June 3	Steamship Queen of the Fal, of Falmouth, assisted to refloat
	Aug 24	Trawler G. V. E. Leonge, of Camaret, stood by
1932	Sep 5	Yachts Spica, Marlin, Osprey, Mathari, Victory and Namouna, of Falmouth, escorted
		Yacht Daedalus, of Plymouth, stood by
	Oct 21	Yacht Jess, saved yacht
1934	Sep 5	Motor boat Ken, of Polruan, saved boat and landed 3
1935	Nov 30	Crew of steamship Orchis, of Bideford, on board fishing vessel, escorted
1940	Jan 4	Steamship Ardangorm, of Glasgow, saved (in two trips 11 and 25) 36
1945	Aug 11	Yacht, of Fowey, saved yacht and 5
1946	July 21	Sailing dinghy, saved dinghy

| | Nov 28 | Steamship Valborg, of Copenhagen, escorted to harbour |

The Brothers Reserve Lifeboat

| 1947 | Mar 23 | Motor vessel Empire Contamar, of London, saved 7 |

C. D. E. C. Lifeboat

1947	July 20	Motor yacht Easting, of Plymouth, saved yacht and 1
1948	Aug 7	Landed a woman who had fallen from cliffs
		Landed three scouts cut off by tide
1949	Aug 28	Motor vessel Thelado, of London, assisted to save
1950	Jan 15	Fishing boat Prim, of Falmouth, and ex-RAF tender, saved 2 craft and 2
	Sep 16	Yacht Black Maria, remoored drifting yacht
1951	Sep 8	Yacht Englyn I, of Southampton, landed 4
1952	Jun 8	Motor boat E. M., saved boat and 1
	Sep 9	Sailing dinghy, of Fowey, saved dinghy and 2
1953	Nov 3	Motor vessel Summity, of London, stood by
1954	July 3	Motor launch Acorn, of Fowey, towed in launch, gave help
	Aug 18	Rowing boat, saved boat and 2
	Sep 2	Fishing boat Ibis, of Mevagissey, stood by and escorted

Deneys Reitz Lifeboat

1953	Mar 23	Motor vessel Festivity, of London, stood by and escorted
	Aug 21	Dinghy Shellduck, of Fowey, saved dinghy and 2
	Sep 25	Sailing boat, saved boat
1956	Mar 16	Motor vessel Eminent, of Amsterdam, landed a sick man and stood by

Cunard Reserve Lifeboat

| 1956 | July 29 | Yacht Fairwood, of London, remoored yacht |

Deneys Reitz Lifeboat

1956	Aug 17	Motor vessel Frode, of Sarpsborg, escorted
	Sep 28	Yacht Ocra, of Scheveningen, saved 3
		Yacht Ocra (second service), saved yacht
	Oct 1	Yacht Corrie, of Southampton, escorted

C. D. E. C. Reserve Lifeboat

| 1957 | Mar 13 | RAF floating target, salved target |

Deneys Reitz Lifeboat

1957	July 7	Motor boat, saved boat and 1
1958	May 3	Reported flashing light, picked up flare
	July 20	Motor yacht Undine, of Plymouth, towed in yacht and 9, gave help
	Sep 12	Girls cut off by tide, landed 2
1960	Mar 18	Yacht Gazelle, of London, saved yacht and 4
	Apr 14	Yacht Irene, of Boston, towed in yacht and 2
1961	July 2	Dinghy Karine, saved dinghy
	11	Harbour Commissioners' launch and 2 dinghies, escorted
		Dinghy Bariola, saved dinghy
	30	Yacht Polyanna, escorted
	Aug 13	Boys cut off by the tide, landed 2
1962	Sep 2	Yacht Why, of Fowey, escorted
1963	Mar 8	Motor vessel Idalith, of Æroskobing, stood by
	July 26	Motor yacht Debbie G, of Fowey, saved yacht & 3
1964	Oct 21	Unsuccessful search for a missing boat
1965	Aug 15	Persons cut off by the tide, saved 2

Cecil and Lilian Philpott Reserve Lifeboat

| 1966 | Apr 9 | Yacht Tormentoso, landed a body |

Deneys Reitz Lifeboat

	May 18	Motor boat, saved boat
	Aug 4	Motor launch Darlwyne, landed 2 bodies
	Sep 2	Yacht Sirocco, of Port Wrinkle, escorted
1967	May 5	Fishing vessel Yves Chantal, of St Malo, saved vessel and 8
	Sep 19	Dinghy, saved dinghy and 2
1968	Apr 14	Two dinghies, escorted
	May 11	Dinghy, saved dinghy
	June 4	Motor boat Heather Glen, of Fowey, gave help
	July 22	Girl stranded on cliff, gave help
	Aug 8	Speedboat, gave help and landed 2
1969	Aug 2	Rubber dinghy, saved dinghy
	Oct 11	Yacht Ziska in tow of motor boat Molly, escorted
		Motor boat Francis Drake, saved boat and 3
1970	Apr 6	Motor vessel Paul Westers, of Groningen, stood by and escorted
	12	Rowing boat, saved boat

John and Lucy Cordingley Reserve Lifeboat

| | May 22 | Motor boat Vi, gave help and landed 4 |
| | Nov 20 | Motor vessel Fixity, of London, stood by |

Deneys Reitz Lifeboat

1972	May 1	Yacht Monza II, in tow of fishing boat, stood by
	14	Motor fishing boat Fiona, of Fowey, saved boat and 2
1974	Aug 9	Various yachts in trouble, escorted yachts
	Sep 21	Schooner yacht Toucan of Lynher, gave help
1975	June 14	Cabin cruiser Dandy Lion, gave help
	July 12	Yacht Tequila, saved yacht and 2
	Dec 1	Motor vessel Elizabeth Boye, gave help
	4	Motor vessel Wildente, landed injured man
1976	Aug 23	Sloop Endeavour, gave help

Jesse Lumb Reserve Lifeboat

| | Nov 14 | Motor boat Mary T, gave help |

Deneys Reitz Lifeboat

1977	Mar 6	Fishing boat Seafarer, escorted
	Apr 11	Motor boat Rig One, gave help
	21	Sloop, saved boat
	July 30	Motor cruiser, landed 2
	May 16	Fishing boat Mancoz, escorted
1978	Jan 5	Fishing boat Nicholine, saved boat and 2
	July 27	Yacht Gallant Girl, gave help
	Oct 30	Rowing boat, saved boat
1979	Apr 24	Fishing boat Red Shank, of Fowey, gave help
	June 24	Yacht Esfani, in tow of motor boat, gave help
	Aug 23	Speedboat, saved boat and 3

Gertrude Lifeboat

1980	May 11	Yacht Itzdafuz, saved boat and 2
	Sep 5	Tug Persuasion, stood by
1981	May 10	Yacht Christina, of Fowey, saved boat
	Aug 7	Fishing boat, gave help
	Sep 19	Yacht Annapurna, escorted boat

Charles Henry Ashley Lifeboat

| 1982 | May 17 | Catamaran Tic Tac, gave help |
| | June 25 | Cabin cruiser, gave help |

Leonore Chilcott Lifeboat

1983	Mar 27	Sailing dinghy, gave help
	July 13	Fishing boat Abraham Cove, landed 2 from another fishing boat
	15	Motor cruiser Peerie Moutie, gave help
	19	Injured man on board Pescado, landed an injured man
	Sep 2	Yacht First Born, escorted vessel
	Oct 21	Yacht Gay Lord, gave help
	Nov 16	Fishing boat, gave help
	30	Injured man on board bulk carrier Lamaria, landed an injured man
1984	Aug 1	Yacht Grey Gander, escorted boat
	Dec 9	Dinghy, saved boat
1985	Apr 5	Sailboard, saved board and 1
	May 7	Dinghy, landed 2

Merchant Navy Relief Lifeboat

	May 14	Motor boat Equalation, gave help
	30	Yacht Elephant, saved boat and 2
	July 13	Yacht Magpie II, saved boat and 1
	Aug 1	Sailing dinghy, saved boat and 2

Leonore Chilcott Lifeboat

	Aug 17	Fishing boat Nichola, gave help
		Coastguard rescue boat, gave help
	Sep 11	Yacht Secret of Troy, gave help
	22	Sick woman on board cargo vessel Patria, took out doctor, landed a sick woman
1986	June 21	Yacht Non Pareil, gave help
	26	Yacht Jillamanda II, saved boat and 2
	Aug 5	Sailing Club rescue boat, escorted boat
	18	Yacht Bounty, escorted boat
	30	Person cut off by tide, saved 1

Amateur Swimming Associations Relief Lifeboat

	Oct 2	Fishing boat Enchantress, gave help
	23	Rubber dinghy, saved boat and 3
		Fishing boat Aquarius, saved boat and 1
	Dec 7	Fishing boat Silvery Sea, escorted boat

Leonore Chilcott Lifeboat

1987	Apr 11	Sailing dinghy, saved boat and 4
	12	Persons cut off by tide, saved 2
	14	Persons cut off by tide at Lantiviet, saved 5
	27	Small commercial fishing boat, gave help
	June 15	Motor cruiser, gave help
	Aug 4	Small commercial fishing boat, gave help
	5	Swimmer, saved 1
	31	Yacht Vreny, saved boat and 3
	Sep 14	Fishing boat, gave help

Thomas Forehead and Mary Rowse II Lifeboat

1988	Mar 11	Fishing vessel Satanic, escorted vessel
	Apr 5	Speedboat White Fire, landed a body and saved 1
	16	Yacht Ondina, of Polruan, escorted boat
	May 4	Yacht Thamanya, gave help
	June 1	Dinghy, escorted boat
	5	Catamaran Spriggan II, gave help
	22	Fishing vessel Marigold, landed 3, saved vessel
	28	Body in sea, landed a body
	July 31	Rubber dinghy, recovered dinghy
	Aug 13	Sailing Club rescue boat, gave help
	26	Yacht Kensa, gave help
		Skin divers, landed 1

Nov 3 Cabin cruiser with yacht in tow, saved 1
Yacht, saved boat

Faithful Forester Relief Lifeboat

1989 Feb 6 Dead body, recovered a body

Thomas Forehead and Mary Rowse II Lifeboat

	Apr 12	Fishing vessel Jon Lee, gave help
	14	Yacht Niana Tidak, gave help
	29	Sailboard, gave help
	May 21	Motor boat, gave help
	27	Motor boat, saved boat
	June 8	Fishing vessel Soisic, saved vessel and 2
	18	Missing youth, gave help
	21	Sailboard, saved board and 1
	July 25	Injured person on board cabin cruiser Scorpio, landed an injured man
	Aug 1	Fishing vessel Sweet Promise, gave help
	30	Woman cut off by the tide, saved 1
	Sep 9	Dinghy, gave help
	10	Fishing vessel in tow of yacht Sea Quest, escorted
	14	Motor boat, escorted boat
	Oct 9	Fishing vessel Dauphan, in collision with fishing vessel Little Fisher, escorted vessel
	Nov 22	Fishing vessel, gave help
1990	Mar 15	Sailing dinghy, saved boat and 1
	Apr 3	Missing man, landed a body

Faithful Forester Relief Lifeboat

	Apr 9	Fishing vessel Le Migrateur, gave help
	May 21	Cabin cruiser Osprey, gave help
	26	Yacht Johanna Lucretia, gave help
	June 7	Fishing boat Palatine, saved boat and 1
	20	Yacht Slipshod, gave help

Thomas Forehead and Mary Rowse II Lifeboat

	July 23	Man cut off by the tide, gave help
	24	Two sailing dinghies, gave help
	29	Tender to yacht Dream Lady, gave help
		Power boat, escorted boat
	Aug 9	Person cut off by the tide, saved 1
	15	Fishing boat, saved boat and 1
	Sep 5	Fishing vessel Julie Anne, gave help
	14	Dinghy, gave help
	Oct 26	Yacht Sybaris, gave help
	Nov 21	Motor boat, gave help
	Dec 20	Motor vessel Volga-4006, landed a sick woman
		Sailboard, saved 1
1991	Mar 22	Fishing vessel Queen Fisher, gave help
	26	Sailing dinghy, landed 3 and saved boat
	29	Yacht Sentinel, gave help
	31	Motor boat, gave help
	Apr 5	Sailboard, landed 1

Faithful Forester Relief Lifeboat

	June 8	Fishing vessel Palatine, saved vessel and 2
	July 25	Yacht Esprie, saved boat

Thomas Forehead and Mary Rowse II Lifeboat

	Aug 10	Motor boat Princess Toscana, escorted boat
	21	Yacht Sanderling II, gave help
	22	Cabin cruiser Challenger, gave help
	Oct 29	Fishing vessel Didier Patrice, gave help
	Nov 6	Fishing vessel Scorpio, escorted vessel
	25	Pilot boat, escorted boat

1992	Jan 15	Yacht St Luke's Crusader, gave help
	31	Cargo vessel Cormorant, stood by vessel
	May 2	Sick man on board fishing vessel August Rose, took out doctor, landed a sick man
	4	Sick man (and a dog) on board yacht Pegandus, saved boat, landed 1 and a dog
	17	Yacht Thistledown, escorted boat
	24	Injured man at Gribbin Head, gave help
	June 19	Sailing dinghy, escorted boat

Faithful Forester Relief Lifeboat

	July 11	Speedboat Touch'n'go, saved boat and 2
	Aug 12	Fishing vessel Satanic, gave help
	24	Two men stranded in Gully, saved 2
	25	Three persons cut off by the tide, gave help
	31	Fishing vessel, recovered wreckage

Thomas Forehead and Mary Rowse II Lifeboat

1993	Jan 17	Yacht Tean Dawn, gave help
	Feb 7	Three persons stranded on cliff, gave help
	Mar 24	Yacht Cramar, gave help
	Apr 18	Injured man at foot of cliff, gave help
	June 3	Cabin cruiser Trojan, gave help
	6	Nine persons stranded on cliff, gave help
	19	Two persons stranded on cliff, saved 2
	July 17	Motor boat, gave help
	25	Two persons stranded off Lantic Bay, gave help
	27	Rubber dinghy, saved 4
	31	Rubber dinghy, gave help
	Aug 5	Sailing dinghy, saved dinghy and landed 2
	15	Child in sea, saved 1
	17	Four persons stranded on cliff, saved 4
	18	Man fallen from cliff, recovered a body
	Sep 1	Two bathers, stood by
	4	Yacht Petit Gris, gave help
	Oct 17	Jet ski, escorted jet ski
1994	Jan 29	Man stranded at Penare Head, gave help
	Feb 14	Fishing vessel Mystique, saved vessel and 3
	20	Fishing vessel Marigold, one person, a dog and craft brought in
	Apr 12	Rubber dinghy, saved boat
	17	Yacht Lytham Green, four persons and craft brought in
	May 17	Fishing vessel Leonora, one person and craft brought in
	June 1	Yacht, six persons and craft brought in
	10	Fishing vessel Magondole, two persons and craft brought in
	11	Motor boat Bye Bye, two and craft brought in
	26	Motor cruiser Scorpio, three persons and craft brought in
	26	Two skin divers, saved 2
	July 23	Sailing dinghy, landed 2 and craft brought in
	31	Cabin cruiser Mavis, two persons and craft brought in
	Aug 4	Fishing boat Acquila, escorted boat
	Oct 6	Cruiser Kamjaro, landed 2 and saved boat
1995	Mar 25	Dinghy, landed 3 and craft brought in

Faithful Forester Relief Lifeboat

	May 14	Fishing boat Mer, one person and craft brought in
	June 4	Speedboat, escorted boat
	28	Fishing vessel Kestrel Queen, three persons and craft brought in

| | Aug 9 | Dinghy, saved boat and 5 |
| | 13 | Injured man on board fishing vessel Didier Patrice, landed an injured man |

Thomas Forehead and Mary Rowse II Lifeboat

	Oct 8	Yacht Morning Starshine, two persons and craft brought in
	Nov 5	Yacht Zarzuela, saved boat and 2
	25	Two children cut off by tide, saved 2
1996	Jan 7	Canoe, saved 1
	May 20	Yacht Fylla, five persons and craft brought in
	June 30	Sailing dinghy, saved craft and 2
	July 11	Dinghy Lucky Lady, four persons and craft brought in
	30	Motor boat Bonita, five persons and craft brought in
	Aug 5	Yacht First Choice, five persons and craft brought in
	22	Man overboard from yacht Timoneer, saved craft and 1
	23	Yacht Gladsome Light, two persons and craft brought in
	Sep 8	Cabin cruiser Dysie, five persons and craft brought in

Earl and Countess Mountbatten of Burma Relief Lifeboat

| 1997 | Jan 16 | Fishing vessel Heather Anne, landed 4 and craft brought in |

Maurice and Joyce Hardy Lifeboat

| | Mar 8 | Two youths cut off by tide, two people brought in – saved by another lifeboat |

Thomas Forehead and Mary Rowse II Relief LB

| | Mar 27 | Rubber dinghy Bonito in tow of fishing vessel Swallow, escorted craft |
| | Apr 5 | Two divers, two people brought in |

Maurice and Joyce Hardy Lifeboat

	Apr 26	Yacht Pourquoi, saved craft and 4
	May 3	Motor boat Ding Bat, two people and craft brought in
	June 11	Harbour work boat Odyssey, landed 2 and craft brought in
	July 26	Yacht Joker, two people and craft brought in
	30	Yacht Oktober Tea, gave help
		Sailboard, saved 1
	31	Motor boat, two people and craft brought in
	Aug 26	Sailboard, saved board and 1
	Sep 25	Canoe, one person brought in
	27	Yacht, one person and craft brought in
1998	May 10	Yacht Petrel, craft brought in
	15	Fishing vessel Maid of Bodinnic, two people and craft brought in
	June 5	Catamaran Sports Page, gave help
		Three people cut off by tide, three brought in
		Yacht Cabo de Hornos, escorted craft
	July 14	Yacht Silent Running, escorted craft
	19	Yacht Flash Dancer, landed 3 and craft brought in
	Aug 8	Yacht Springer, two people and craft brought in
	18	Yacht Moonshine, four people & craft brought in
	20	Yacht Gift of the Shadows, escorted craft
	23	Sailing dinghy, saved craft and 1

	Sep 10	Yacht Kerenza, saved craft and 6
1999	Mar 27	Yacht Ocean Sunrise, three people and craft brought in
	Apr 17	Yacht Wight Gambit, gave help
	May 2	Fishing vessel Talisman, three people and craft brought in

Dora Foster McDougall Relief Lifeboat

	June 27	Catamaran Jade D, saved craft and 1
	Aug 6	Yacht Locean, one person and craft brought in
	9	Fowey inshore lifeboat, landed 3 and craft brought in
	14	Yacht Ocean Sunrise, gave help
	Sep 13	Yacht Milky Whey, two people and craft brought in
	24	Injured man on board fishing vessel Sormovskiy 3057, gave help
	Oct 1	Fishing vessel Mary Eilleen, landed 1 and craft brought in
	9	Yacht Tonatiuh, three people and craft brought in
	26	Yacht Irene Jack, four people and craft brought in
2000	Jan 8	Fishing vessel Valerie May, saved craft and 2

Maurice and Joyce Hardy Lifeboat

	Jan 10	Fishing vessel Cornish Lass, landed 2 and saved vessel
	Mar 25	Inflatable dinghy, landed 3, craft brought in
	June 3	Dinghy, gave help
	18	Four people cut off by the tide, landed 2
	July 9	Yacht Rivalee, escorted vessel
	Aug 5	Yacht Curlew, two people and craft brought in
	18	Yacht Noatun, three people and craft brought in
	25	Yacht Daydream III, escorted vessel
	Dec 20	Fishing vessel Valerie May, saved craft and 2
2001	Mar 2	Fishing vessel Saturn, gave help
		Fishing vessel My Tara, landed 3, craft brought in
	15	Yacht Pochad, two people and craft brought in
	24	Catamaran Ton Ton Milot, landed 2 and craft brought in
	May 11	Power boat Galene of Cork, landed 2 and craft brought in
	29	Injured woman, stood by
	June 12	Power boat Quiver, four people and craft brought in
	Aug 20	Swimmer, assisted to save one person
	29	Three people stranded on rocks, gave help
	Sep 8	Capsize, gave help
		Injured man on board sail yacht Persuasion V, landed 1
2002	Feb 2	Merchant vessel Kodima, stood by
	14	Fishing vessel Cornish Maiden, landed 2 and craft brought in
	Mar 27	Person cut off by tide, one person brought in
	June 26	People cut off by the tide, stood by
	Aug 3	Tender to pleasure craft Boadicea, landed 5 and craft brought in
	8	Inflatable dinghy, craft brought in
	9	Yacht Harvard, three persons and craft brought in
	Sep 8	Cabin cruiser Fosse, landed 2 and saved craft
	26	Missing person, stood by
	Nov 7	Fishing vessel Venus, two persons and craft brought in

2003	Jan 16	Fishing vessel Renown, three people and craft brought in
	Mar 31	Yacht Cosima, two people and craft brought in
	Apr 1	Yacht Kipenzi, one person and craft brought in
	6	Powered boat, gave help
		Powered boat Gadfly, three people and craft brought in
	18	Tender to pleasure craft, four people brought in
	May 18	Yacht Lady In Red, four people and craft brought in
	22	Yacht Ellen Grace, two people and craft brought in
	28	Yacht La Trek, two people and craft brought in
	June 19	Yacht Aldarion, one person and craft brought in
	July 1	Motor boat Dad's Boat, one person and craft brought in
		Cabin cruiser Black Morwenna, two people and craft brought in
	4	Person cut off by the tide, stood by
	11	Speed boat The Phoenix, landed 1 and saved craft
	13	Powered boat Ebb Tide, escorted craft
		RIB, landed 2 and craft brought in
	20	Powerboat, escorted craft
	21	Yacht Doublet, three people and craft brought in
	27	Dory, two people brought in
		Yacht Galea, gave help
		Yacht Merryden, three people & craft brought in
	Aug 2	Power boat Sandy, five people & craft brought in
	8	Motor boat Amy, landed 1
	10	Yacht Blue Ribbon, stood by
	20	Powerboat Cormorant, five people brought in
	25	Seven people cut off by tide, gave help
	Nov 16	Fishing vessel, One person and craft brought in
2004	May 16	Sick woman, landed 1
	18	Person in the sea, gave help
	June 20	Tender, gave help – located and passed tender
	July 30	Fishing vessel Jessica Grace, escorted craft
	Aug 1	Powered boats, gave help
	2	Body board, landed 2
		Inflatable dinghy, landed 2
		Rowing boat, landed 1
	3	Yacht Vinca 2, one person and craft brought in
2005	Feb 6	Injured man, landed 1
	11	Yacht Mystic Wind, saved 2
	Mar 6	Fishing vessel Mystique, two persons and craft brought in
	22	Powered boat, two persons and craft brought in
	May 1	Sick man on board yacht Sathuta, gave help
	8	Powered boat, two persons and craft brought in
	July 6	Yacht, four persons brought in
	7	Yacht Rhythmic Beat, two persons and craft brought in
	20	Sailing dinghy, one person brought in
	Aug 13	Fishing vessel Isis, one person and craft brought in
	15	Injured person on Lantic Beach, landed 1
	28	Powered boat, five persons and craft brought in

	Oct 16	Yacht Seafarer 2, four persons and craft brought in
	Nov 2	Cargo vessel Galina, stood by
	Dec 15	Divers missing from diving support craft, three persons and craft brought in
2006	Apr 15	Yacht Aguila, gave help – illuminated scene
	July 2	Yacht Sombra, one person and craft brought in
	Aug 3	Inflatable dinghy, four persons and craft brought in
	9	Powered boat, five persons and craft brought in
	10	Yacht Sonny, one person and craft brought in
	12	Inflatable dinghy, stood by
		Fowey inshore lifeboat, three persons and craft brought in
	Sep 13	Missing person, landed a body
	Dec 24	Fishing vessel Crimson Tide, one person and craft brought in
2007	Mar 25	Fishing vessel Atlanta 2, three persons and craft brought in
	Apr 2	People stranded, eight persons brought in
	May 12	Yacht Gentoo Of Ardwell, two persons and craft brought in
	19	Diver support craft Morning Glory, gave help – administered first aid and assisted to helicopter
	June 8	Person at risk, one person brought in
	13	Yacht Forever Changes, seven persons and craft brought in
	Aug 4	Injured woman, landed 1
	5	Fishing vessel Aquilla, 11 persons and craft brought in
	14	Children cut off by the tide, landed 2
	16	Powered boat, craft brought in
	18	Sailing dinghy, escorted craft
	25	Powered boat, gave help – administered first aid
	Sep 5	Yacht Siliwen, one person and craft brought in
	Oct 15	Fishing vessel Natalie, one person brought in
2008	Apr 17	Injured man on board fishing vessel Roseanne, saved 1
	May 3	People cut off by tide, landed 3
	14	Yacht Thursdays Child, landed 1, two people and craft brought in
	July 19	Powered boat Southern Comfort, two people and craft brought in
	23	Yacht Azsnor, four people and craft brought in
	Aug 3	Person on Mevagissey pier, stood by
	8	Yacht Carousel, four people and craft brought in
	10	Powered boat Kerry Anne, escorted craft
	12	Powered boat, landed 2 and craft brought in
	14	Tender, one person brought in
		Powered boat, one person brought in
		Powered boat, eight people and craft brought in
	20	Yacht Demelza, five people and craft brought in
	23	Powered boat Justified Expense, two people and craft brought in
	30	People cut off by tide, gave help

Personnel

Honorary Secretaries

William E. Geach	1859 – 1898
Herbert E. Cooke	1898 – 1908
William Henry Polglaze	1908 – 9.1921
K. G. Spratt	1.1922 – 12.1944
Major D. R. Carter	12.1945 – 1966
Capt J. G. Wilson	1.1967 – 1983
Capt J. R. Pritchard	1983 – 10.2000
Capt Samuel Guy	10.2000 – 2005
Capt William P. Mitchell	3.11.2005 –

Coxswains

Joshua Heath	1859 – 1882
John Bennett	1882 – 1895
Samuel Ashton	8.1894 – 9.1910
Edwin Charles Bennet	9.1910 – 10.1917
William Cauker	10.1917 – 9..1922
John H. Grose	1922 – 3.1934
John Watters	3.1934 – 10.1959
James Turpin	10.1959 – 1977
Brian Willis	1978 – 1989
Matthew Keith Stuart (joint Cox/Mech)	7.1989 –

Mechanics (at Fowey)

L. W. Thomas	1928 – 1930
William McDonald	1930 – 3.1958
Frederick G. Webber	3.1958 – 6.1982
Matthew Keith Stuart (joint Cox/Mech)	June 1982 –

Second Coxswains

William Robins	8.1894 – 9.1910
George Bishop	10.1910 – 9.1917
Sidney Robins	9.1917 – 9.1922
Wallace Stephens	
Bill Stephens	
Alfie Barron	
Brian Willis	
Nicky Elliot	
Matthew Keith Stuart	– 7.1989
Steve Barker	7.1989 –

RNLI

◀ Keith Stuart, who was appointed Coxswain in July 1989. Originally from Amble, where served on the lifeboat crew from 1975, he was appointed mechanic at Fowey in June 1982. He took over as Coxswain from Brian Willis, who had to retire two years early for health reasons. (Tim Stevens)

Ex Lifeboats

The ex lifeboat rally held at Fowey has become a regular fixture on the town's summer calendar. It is an opportunity for the owners of former lifeboats to gather at the port for the weekend, meet old friends and show off their restored lifeboats, which are immaculately maintained and the pride of their owners.

The first rally was held in 1998, when the old Looe pulling lifeboat Ryder, which had been completely restored, and the almost entirely unaltered 46ft Watson motor lifeboat Michael Stephens came together and were opened up to the public. They were joined the following year Gertrude, privately owned in Mevagissey, and the pilot boat Treffry, a former Thames class lifeboat owned by Fowey Harbour Commissioners.

From these humble beginnings the rally has grown to become an annual event attended by many old lifeboats. The main aim of the rally is to raise funds for the RNLI, and it has sometimes coincided with the station's lifeboat day. An increasing number of boats have attended, including some from as far as Northern Ireland. The boats were moored at the Albert Quay pontoon during the first rallies, but Berrill's Yard pontoon has been the venue for the last few years.

▼ Several ex lifeboats moored together on the east side of the river at the end of the 2003 event. (Nicholas Leach)

▶ The former Looe pulling lifeboat Ryder, built in 1902 and now based at Polperro, puts to sea during the 2006 rally, with a crew of volunteers at the oars finding out the effort and hard work involved in nineteenth and early twentieth century life-saving. (Nicholas Leach)

▶ The former St Mary's 46ft 9in Watson class lifeboat Guy and Clare Hunter, which also served temporarily at Fowey, was in attendance at the 2003 rally having come from her home base of Strangford Lough in Northern Ireland. (Nicholas Leach)

▶ One of the regular attendees at the ex lifeboat rallies has been the former 48ft 6in Solent lifeboat Douglas Currie, which is usually based at Portishead. She was built in 1973 and sold out of service in 1992 having served at Kirkwall, Macduff, Fraserburgh, Portpatrick and Workington. (Nicholas Leach)

Donkey Summer Fair

Sunday
15th August
10am - 4pm

PROGRAMME
& MAP £1

Thanks for visiting!
Enjoy your donkey day!

In aid of The Donkey Sanctuary & EST

Zone J
EST Centre

Cakes, Quality Bric-a-Brac, Tombola,
Bouncy Castle, Books, Silent Auction,
Splat the Rat and more games!
Refreshments inc. Tea, Coffee & Cakes

Car Park

**Zone K
Main Arena**

**Zone H
Craft Marquee**

Zone K - Main Arena

10.30am - Dog Agility
11.30am - Gymkhana by children from EST
followed by Riding Award Ceremony
1pm - Dog Agility
2pm - Egg Throwing
3pm - EST Grand Raffle Draw
3.30pm - Egg Throwing Final

Fun Zone

Tea Cup Ride
Inflatable Assault Course
Candy Floss
Bucking Bronco
Announcement Unit
(Lost Children)
More Stalls

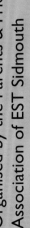

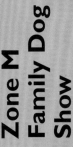

Zone M
Family Dog
Show
1.30pm onwards
Organised by the Parents & Friends
Association of EST Sidmouth

Maze

Restaurant
Food served all day

Zone E
Box 16
Overseas Exhibition

Zone I
EST Drive
BBQ
Adopt a Donkey
(Win a hamper)
Plant Stall
Skittles
Coconut Shie

Welcome to our largest fundraising event of the year - the Donkey Summer Fair! We are delighted to have your support and wish you a wonderful time with your family here today.

All monies raised during this event will help fund the general work of The Donkey Sanctuary and our connected charity, The Elisabeth Svendsen Trust for Children and Donkeys (EST). 100% of the takings from all charity-run stalls* will be used to support our work and, of course, any donation you give today, no matter how small, will be gratefully received.

Have a great time and if you have any questions, please feel free to ask any of the staff or volunteers who will endeavour to assist you.

Yours truly,

Dr Elisabeth D Svendsen, MBE
Founder of The Donkey Sanctuary & EST

*Commercial participants are charged for their pitches.

Other ways you can help us fundraise today:

1 - Adopt a Donkey. Sign up today at the Adopt a Donkey Stand and you could win a jam-packed goodies hamper.

2 - Make a one-off donation. Any donation, no matter how small, will be gratefully received.

3 - Buy something from our Gift Shop. From a donkey diary to a donkey umbrella, there is something for everyone.

FAMILY DOG SHOW (Zone M)

from 1.30pm. Classes (£1 per entry):

1. Best Puppy under 12 months
2. Prettiest Bitch
3. Most Handsome Dog
4. Best Young Handler
5. Waggiest Tail sponsored by Wagg
6. Most Appealing Eyes
7. Best Dog under 18"
8. Best Dog over 18"
9. Best Veteran over 8 years
10. Best Rescue
11. Fastest 'Bonio' Eater sponsored by Purina
12. Best Condition
13. Fancy Dress
14. Best In Show - All First Prize Winners

Going on holiday?
You can also visit our sanctuaries in Cyprus, Ireland, Italy and Spain.
Visit - **www.thedonkeysanctuary.org**

Grand Raffle Tickets

Purchase a grand raffle ticket from the main Craft Tent (Zone H) or EST Centre (Zone J). Draw takes place at 3pm in the Main Arena (zone K).

Today's Housekeeping Rules!

Please do not feed the donkeys
Please refrain from feeding the donkeys as it encourages them to bite. We have buckets in the Visitors' Centre and the EST Slade Centre where you can place the donkeys' favourite treats so they can be shared out equally.

No smoking
We would ask that you refrain from smoking whilst at The Donkey Sanctuary because of the obvious dangers of hay and straw being set alight.

Children
Parents are responsible for their children and must supervise them at all times. If you have 'lost' your child, please report the matter to the PA unit located in the Marquee Field (Zone L).

Hand Washing Facilities
We recommend that you wash your hands after handling the donkeys, especially before eating. Washing facilities can be found in the Main Yard and in the toilet blocks and hand sanitisers are available throughout the site.

TIMED EVENTS AT A GLANCE!

10.30am	Dog Agility **Zone K**	
	Book Signing by Dr Svendsen **Zone H**	
11.15am	Farrier Display **Zone D**	
11.30am	Gymkhana Riding Display and Awards **Zone K**	
	Punch & Judy **Zone C**	
1.00pm	Dog Agility **Zone K**	
	Donkey Cart rides **Zone B**	
1.15pm	Farrier Display **Zone D**	
1.30pm	Family Dog Show **Zone M**	
	Punch & Judy **Zone C**	
2.00pm	Book Signing by Dr Svendsen **Zone H**	
	Egg Challenge **Zone K**	
3.00pm	Punch & Judy **Zone C**	
	EST Grand Raffle Draw **Zone K**	
3.30pm	Egg Challenge Final **Zone K**	

These are the start times only

The Hayloft Restaurant

Our restaurant has a new menu, longer opening hours and all profits go to the donkeys. Why not pick up a loyalty card today and pop up regularly for superb, locally sourced food and drink?

Our Forthcoming Events

Christmas Craft Fair
Sunday 14th November
10am to 4pm at The Donkey Sanctuary

Candlelight Evening
Friday 10th December
3.30pm onwards at The Donkey Sanctuary (carol service at 5pm)

EST Christmas Fair
Saturday 4th December
10am to 3pm at EST Sidmouth

£2 Trailer Rides will be running throughout the day from Zone A, Main Drive.

Zone B
Hospital Padd[ock]

1pm to 3pm - Donkey C[art]
(£2 per Cart Ride)

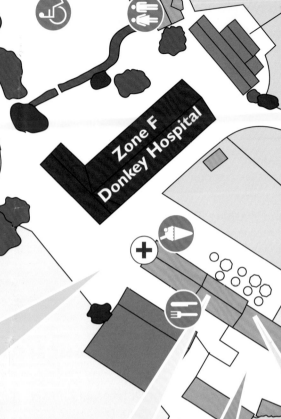

Zone F
Donkey Hospital

Zone A
Main Drive

Donkey Lorry, Bric-a-Brac Stall, Heart FM, Air Cadets, Police, Fire Brigade, Trailer Rides (£2) and Charlotte the Antique Organ

 First Aid Point

 Toilets

Ice Cream

Catering

Car Park

Visitors' Centre & Gift Shop

Zone D
Main Yard

11.15am ⎱ Farrier Displays
1.15pm ⎰
Horse Racing
Knitted Goods Stall

Disabled Car Park

Hospital Paddocks

ck
rt Rides

Car Park

Zone C
Shelter One/Children's Corner

11.30am
1.30pm } Punch & Judy
3.00pm

Face Painting, Tattoo Transfers, Glitter Tattoo Transfers, Bouncy Castle, Hair Braiding, Carrot Game and Football Game

Zone H - Craft Marquee

10.30am to 12.00noon } Dr Svendsen
2pm to 2.30pm } Book Signing

Donkey Sanctuary Gifts and Merchandise Stalls including high quality Bric-a-Brac, Crafts, Books, Jewellery and African Gifts

FREE PRIZE DRAW

Win a £50 Next Voucher!

Kindly donated by Next's Exeter store.

For your chance to win, please complete the enclosed entry form and post it in the "Free Prize Draw" box located in the EST Slade Centre (Zone J) or the Visitors' Centre.

The winner will be notified in writing.

The Donkey Sanctuary

The Donkey Sanctuary aims to protect donkeys and mules and promote their welfare worldwide. We are actively working in 14 countries and have 10 farms in the UK and Ireland where thousands of donkeys are cared for.

EST

The Elisabeth Svendsen Trust for Children and Donkeys

EST provides donkey-riding therapy to children with special needs and disabilities, and pays visits to the elderly in the local community. Our centres are found in Birmingham, Ivybridge, Leeds, Manchester and of course here, within the grounds of the Sanctuary.

Sidmouth, Devon, EX10 0NU

www.thedonkeysanctuary.org.uk

www.elisabethsvendsentrust.org.uk